SEAMUS HEANEY

Faber Student Guides

SEAMUS HEANEY

Neil Corcoran

faber and faber
LONDON · BOSTON

First published in 1986
by Faber and Faber Limited
3 Queen Square London WC1N 3AU

Printed in Great Britain by
Redwood Burn Ltd Trowbridge Wiltshire
All rights reserved

British Library Cataloguing in Publication Data

Corcoran, Neil
Seamus Heaney: students' guide.
1. Heaney, Seamus —— Criticism and
interpretation
I. Title
821'.914   PR6058.E2Z/

ISBN 0-571-13955-8

Library of Congress Cataloging-in-Publication Data

Corcoran, Neil.
Seamus Heaney.
(A Faber student guide)
Bibliography: p.
1. Heaney, Seamus—Criticism and interpretation.
I. Title   II. Series.
PR6058.E2Z6   1986   821'.914   86-11516
ISBN 0-571-13955-8 (pbk)

For my mother

The Faber Student Guides

In an age when critical theory promises, or threatens, to 'cross over' into literature and to become its own object of study, there is a powerful case for re-asserting the primacy of the literary text. The Faber Student Guides are intended in the first instance to provide substantial critical introductions to writers of major importance. Although each contributor inevitably writes from a considered critical position, it is not the aim of the series to impose a uniformity of theoretical approach. Each Guide will make use of biographical material and each will conclude with a select bibliography which will in all cases take note of the latest developments usefully relevant to the subject. Beyond that, however, contributors have been chosen for their critical abilities as well as for their familiarity with the subject of their choice.

Although the primary aim of the series is to focus attention on individual writers, there will be exceptions. Among our future plans are studies of the fiction of the First and Second World Wars; and of Edwardian drama. And although the majority of writers or periods studied will be of the twentieth century, this is not intended to preclude other writers or periods – as the study of Emily Dickinson shows. Above all, the series aims to return readers to a sharpened awareness of those texts without which there would be no criticism.

John Lucas

Contents

Preface

I intend this book primarily as a commentary on
Seamus Heaney's poems which may help the reader
better to understand and appreciate them. I have been
aware, therefore, of the need to convey a considerable
amount of explanatory material – on matters of Irish
history and politics, for instance, and on Heaney's
allusions (since his work is full of other literature, and
I believe what he tells us in 'The Makings of a Music':
that the 'whole lift' of a passage may be increased by
the knowledge of an allusion). But I hope that my
attempts at explication are always enlivened by critical
interpretation and evaluation; and I intend that the
book should enforce and defend my sense of Seamus
Heaney as the most significant poet now writing in
English.

I am grateful to John Byrne and Paul Driver for
showing me some fugitive Heaney material I might not
otherwise have seen; and to my wife Gillian for every-
thing else.

I am also most grateful to Seamus Heaney himself
for allowing me to quote, in Chapter I, from conver-
sations I had with him in Dublin on 5 and 6 July 1985.
Everything that appears without direct citation in that
chapter is taken from a recording of those conversations,
as is some of the incidental information about the
'Station Island' sequence contained in Chapter VI.
Although I have not used footnotes, everything else

cited in my text is included in the bibliography.

Neil Corcoran
Sheffield, November 1985

I

In Between: On Seamus Heaney's Life

> Two buckets were easier carried than one.
> I grew up in between.
>
> My left hand placed the standard iron weight.
> My right tilted a last grain in the balance.
>
> Baronies, parishes met where I was born.
> When I stood on the central stepping stone
>
> I was the last earl on horseback in midstream
> Still parleying, in earshot of his kernes.
>
> 'Terminus' (from *Hailstones*)

One definition of 'Irish' that I liked a lot was Samuel Beckett's. When he was interviewed by a French journalist, the journalist said: 'Vous êtes Anglais, Monsieur Beckett?' To which Beckett replied: 'Au contraire'.

> Seamus Heaney to Frank Kinahan, 1982

Seamus Heaney was born on 13 April 1939, to Patrick and Margaret Kathleen (née McCann) Heaney, on a farm called Mossbawn, in the townland of Tamniarn, Co. Derry, Northern Ireland. He was the eldest of nine children, two girls and seven boys. His father, in addition to farming the fifty-acre Mossbawn, also worked as a cattle dealer. From 1945 to 1951 Heaney attended the local Anahorish School, and from 1951 to 1957 he went as a boarder to St Columb's College in

Derry city, about forty miles from his home. When he was fourteen, the family moved from the Mossbawn farm to a farm at the other end of the parish called The Wood, on which Heaney's father had been brought up, and which he had now inherited from an uncle. Heaney believes that a contributory factor in the decision to move when they did was probably the death at the time, in a road accident close to the house, of one of his brothers, Christopher – the incident commemorated in one of his earliest poems, 'Mid-Term Break'.

The move to The Wood seems definitively to have sealed off the world of Heaney's childhood: in his prose recollections, it is the 'kindly' name of Mossbawn which stands guardian over that first, given world, the world he instinctively returned to for the material of most of his earliest poems. 'Mossbawn' is also the title of two poems which dedicate his fourth book, *North*, to his aunt, Mary Heaney, who lived with the family. Her position in Heaney's early life was clearly a very significant one:

She was the affectionate centre. I'm not saying in any way that my mother was distant, she was just always so busy with children; but Mary's function was almost entirely benign. She was the heart of the house in some ways, and as a child I was 'petted' on her, as they say. There were two women, as it were, in my life – happily there. Mary was always there as a kind of second mother, really.

Everything Heaney has himself written about his childhood reinforces the sense of intimate domestic warmth and affection as its prevailing atmosphere. It is a quality which Heaney's wife, Marie, envied when she first came across it:

His family life was utterly together, like an egg contained within the shell, without any quality of otherness, without the sense of loss that this otherness brings. They

[12]

had confidence in the way they lived, a lovely impeccable confidence in their own style.

quoted in Polly Devlin, *All Of Us There*, p. 17

This 'togetherness' inside the walls of the home was not reflected, however, in the world beyond those walls, where everything spoke, on the contrary, of division. This was, first of all, a matter of the accident of local topography:

> From the beginning I was very conscious of boundaries. There was a drain or stream, the Sluggan drain, an old division that ran very close to our house. It divided the townland of Tamniarn from the townland of Anahorish and those two townlands belonged in two different parishes, Bellaghy and Newbridge, which are also in two different dioceses: the diocese of Derry ended at the Sluggan drain and the diocese of Armagh began. I was always going backwards and forwards. I went to school in Anahorish School, so I learnt the Armagh catechism; but I belonged, by birth and enrolment, to Bellaghy parish. So I didn't go with the rest of the school to make my first communion in Newbridge. And when I was confirmed in Bellaghy, the bishop had to ask us these ritual questions and I didn't know the Derry catechism. When we moved to the other end of the parish when I was fourteen, I still played football for Castledawson, though I was living in the Bellaghy team's district. I seemed always to be a little displaced; being in between was a kind of condition, from the start.

What begins there as a description of topographical division shades inevitably into the greater divisions of Heaney's childhood in Northern Ireland: the interwoven divisions of religion and culture (Heaney's 'football' is Gaelic football, played exclusively by the Catholic minority). In the essay '1972', collected in *Preoccupations*, this consciousness of division leads him to derive from the name 'Mossbawn' itself, with its

Scots and possibly Gaelic etymology, 'a metaphor of the split culture of Ulster'. The actual location of the farm – between Toomebridge where the rebel Rody McCorley was hanged in 1798, and Castledawson, the estate of the Chichester-Clarkes, a leading Unionist family – Heaney thinks of as placing him, symbolically for a Northern Catholic, between the marks of nationalist local sentiment and the marks of colonial and British presence, between the 'bog' and the 'demesne'. Although his first school, Anahorish, took both Catholics and Protestants, and although religious differences in this rural community were usually pragmatically sub-merged in the interests of the business of agriculture, everything in Heaney's first world bore the imprint of the fact that he was born a Catholic in the North of Ireland.

There were, firstly, the liturgical and popular forms of the religion itself: the Mass, confessions, the family rosary, the recitation of the catechism, and the numer-ous small pieties of an earlier phase of Irish Catholi-cism, which supplied an entire context for a life. There was the sense of an intercessory feminine presence in human affairs fostered by the veneration of Mary. There was that 'sacramental' sense of the landscape described in 'The Sense of Place' in *Preoccupations*, the vestigial presence of an older 'magical' or 'marvellous' view of the world which survived in rituals such as the plaiting of Brigid's Crosses, the gathering of flowers for May altars, the turnip-candles of Hallowe'en. It was a disappearing world in which, Heaney has said in his essay 'The Poet as a Christian', 'we never felt ourselves alone in the universe for a second'. Perhaps most sig-nificant for his own future work were the rituals at-tendant on death:

My childhood was full of death: only the first couple of times scary and strange. Two of my grandparents, and lots of granduncles and aunts died when I was quite young and I went to the wakes and funerals. Then, since I was the eldest, in my early teens I used to represent the family at some funerals and the sight of a corpse and the whole ritual were quite common to me. It's a big social engagement, everyone comes to the house. Neighbours would sit up all night, and one or two of the family. This business of sitting all night in the wake-house, it's inscrutable as the Red Indians, an inner system of courtesy and honour and obligement. So I took all that as just an ordinary fact of life. I'm certain all those funerals and corpses had some definite effect, and I remember after writing 'The Tollund Man' I began to think if I were to go to an analyst, he would certainly link the outlined and pacified and *rigor mortis* face of the Tollund man with all that submerged life and memory.

But being a Catholic in Northern Ireland extended, and extends, far beyond the forms of the religion itself: as Heaney defined it in an interview in the *Guardian* (2 November 1974), 'It's almost a racist term, a label for a set of cultural suppositions.' It meant that the reading matter of Heaney's childhood included, as well as English comics and adventure stories, Irish nationalist publications too – the *Wolfe Tone Annual*, for instance, with its celebrations of the fact and spirit of the 1798 rebellion against English rule in Ireland. Such material, and the singing of Irish patriotic songs within the family, created for Heaney, as for most members of the Catholic minority, a mythology profoundly at odds with the dominant Unionist culture of the North. This mythology, fostered by an early reading of Celtic heroic stories and by his study of the Irish language for six years at school, gave him a radical sense of being Irish in a state which considered itself British. Heaney's own family was pacifically nationalist rather than more aggressively republican; but it has been abundantly clear, since 1968, what real political grievances were inherent in these 'cultural suppositions'. Even prior to the late 1960s, what Heaney has called, in an interview with Monie Begley, the 'silent awarenesses' of religious and cultural division, became articulate every so often: when, for instance, the drums of the twelfth of July – the Loyalist celebration of the battle of the Boyne – filled the air with their intimidating noise; when one of Heaney's brothers was beaten up after attending a republican meeting; and when Heaney himself experienced the usual aggravations of the minority, being stopped regularly at roadblocks in the 1950s by RUC patrols and by his armed and uniformed neighbours acting in their capacity as the B-Special Constabulary (incidents which lie behind 'The Ministry of Fear' in *North*).

The social forms of Heaney's early life were exclusively Catholic: the church, the Gaelic football team and the Catholic village hall were the sole congregating places for a small rural community. His secondary education, at a Catholic boarding school which also served as the diocesan seminary, powerfully enforced the religious and cultural context:

There was the sense of a common culture about the place; we were largely Catholic farmers' sons being taught by farmers' sons. The idea of a religious vocation was in the air all the time; not a coercion by any means, but you would have to be stupid or insensitive not to feel the invitation to ponder the priesthood as a destiny. However, in the first year, the way people separated themselves was that those who came with notions of the priesthood would choose Greek and the others chose French. So I chose French.

In attending St Columb's, Heaney was one of the earliest beneficiaries of the 1947 Education Act, which made a proper secondary education a possibility for the small rural farming class Heaney came from, and for the repressed urban working class of Northern Ireland. In eventually supplying, for the first time, an educated, professional Catholic middle class in the North, this act may be considered largely responsible for the release of political energy there in the 1960s. In addition to Heaney, St Columb's has produced a number of other leading figures in the public and cultural life of modern Ireland, including Seamus Deane, John Hume, Eamonn McCann and Brian Friel:

> We certainly had some sense of capacity about us. The school was very much geared to getting you through the exams, very academically pitched, and very good *at* that. Some of the teachers were terrifically dedicated people. We were tuned like violins to play the tune of the exams.

Having successfully played his own tune, Heaney went to Queen's University, Belfast in 1957 to read English Language and Literature, and graduated with a first class honours degree in 1961. His awareness of a 'split culture' took on a new meaning at the university, as he attempted to hold in some kind of balance the sophistications of a modern literary education and the received ideas and impressions of his childhood. Unlike many university students who have found themselves, for one reason or another, in a broadly comparable position, Heaney did retain a genuine loyalty to the home culture. In *Among Schoolchildren* he tells us that, as well as attending university sherry parties on the Malone Road in Belfast, he also joined the Bellaghy Pioneer Total Abstinence Association; as well as reading Shakespeare and Oscar Wilde, he was also a member of the Bellaghy Dramatic Society, 'playing Robert Emmet in a one-act melodrama and having my performance hailed in the crowded columns of the *Mid-Ulster Mail*'; as well as discussing loss of faith in

Victorian literature, he was driving his mother to evening devotions and attending at the exposition of the Blessed Sacrament. This gap between parish and academy was to be bridged eventually by his reading of Daniel Corkery's once-revolutionary study of eighteenth-century Gaelic poetry, *The Hidden Ireland* (1924), and, pre-eminently, of James Joyce.

Of the English literature he read at the university, Heaney was most drawn to what he has described to James Randall as 'poetry with a thrilling physical texture' – Webster, Keats and Hopkins. The latter is certainly the almost risibly obvious presence behind a stanza from a poem written at university which he prints in the essay 'Feeling into Words' in *Preoccupations*:

> Starling thatch-watches, and sudden swallow
> Straight breaks to mud-nest, home-rest rafter
> Up past dry dust-drunk cobwebs, like laughter
> Ghosting the roof of bog-oak, turf-sod and rods of willow.

It is worth noting, nevertheless, that this is not constructed only of what Heaney disparages as 'frail bucolic images', but that it already contains those much sturdier substances, redolent of a real landscape and a real history, the 'turf-sod' which makes its next appearance in 'Digging', and the 'bog-oak' which gets a poem to itself in *Wintering Out*. Although Heaney published one or two such poems in the university magazines *Gorgon* and *Q*, under the pseudonym 'Incertus' ('uncertain, a shy soul fretting and all that', as 'Feeling into Words' has it), he had no sense of contemporary poetry while he was a student, and it seemed impossible to locate any literary life in Belfast.

In the year after leaving Queen's, Heaney did a postgraduate teachers' training diploma at St Joseph's College of Education in Andersonstown, Belfast. This may sound a relatively unambitious course, in those days of opportunity and a reasonable level of funding in British universities, for someone who has just taken a first in English; and, indeed, other possibilities were canvassed:

> I always had this notion that I was going to be a secondary school teacher, living the generic life of the newly upwardly mobile eleven-plus Catholic; it was a very passive, conveyor-belt sense of things. But Peter Butter, who was chairman of the English Department then, suggested a studentship at Balliol, or certainly some graduate work at Oxford, and I remember just being bewildered, and my father and mother had absolutely no sense of that. They wouldn't have stopped me, I'm not saying that, but the world I was moving in didn't have any direction for them, the compass needle just *wobbled*. Butter was very encouraging and urged me to do it, but I suppose there was just some lack of confidence, and lack of *nous*, and lack of precedent. I suppose, too, that there was *some* expectation that I would earn, just because of that traditional shape of life – pay something back to the home, you know. So that moment passed.

During his year at St Joseph's, Heaney did write, as one of the requirements of his diploma, an extended essay on literary magazines in the North of Ireland since 1900. This introduced him to some of the important literary and cultural holdings of the Linen Hall Library in Belfast, and to the work of the contemporary Ulster poet, John Hewitt. Heaney considers this 'the glimmering of link-in, the glimmering that writing could occur on your own doorstep'. He also bought Robin Skelton's anthology, *Six Irish Poets*, in which he encountered, for the first time, some contemporary work from the Republic, in particular the poems of Thomas Kinsella, John Montague and Richard Murphy; and he began to read Ted Hughes. These poets, Heaney has written in the preface to a limited edition of his work (*Poems and a Memoir*, 1982), were 'more in tune with the actual voices of my own first world than the ironies and elegances of MacNeice and Eliot ever could have been. At last I had discovered sounds in print that connected with the world below and beyond print I had known early on in Co. Derry.'

In 1962 he started teaching at St Thomas's Intermediate School (the Ulster name for what, in England, was then known as a 'secondary modern school') in Ballymurphy, Belfast. The headmaster there was Michael McLaverty, the short-story writer, and he introduced Heaney to the poetry of Patrick Kavanagh, lending him *The Great Hunger* (1942) and *A Soul for Sale* (1947). With their rural setting in Co. Monaghan, these books reflected an experience very close to Heaney's own, and Kavanagh was to become one of the major points of literary reference for him. As he told Caroline Walsh, Kavanagh's great achievement was 'to make our subculture – the rural outback – a cultural resource for us all; to give us images of ourselves'. At this time too Heaney's persistent academic interests led him to register, for a year, for a part-time postgraduate degree in Queen's. He had a thesis on Wordsworth's educational ideas in mind:

> I was just floundering really, but there was that kind of neediness and that little sense of destiny which comes with getting a first: that was certainly taken in. And I suppose then the poetry came rushing in as a kind of gap-filler: I felt, well, I didn't do this, and I didn't do that, but maybe I can do this.

Under the compulsion of this 'neediness', and under the direction of these new influences and exemplars, Heaney began to write in 1962. In November of that year his first poem, 'Tractors', which he disparages now as 'an anxious piece about tractors "gargling sadly astride furrows"', was published in the *Belfast Telegraph*, and shortly afterwards poems were taken by other Irish journals. Especially encouraging was the *Kilkenny Magazine* which, from 'down in the great unknown in the South', took 'Mid-Term Break' early in 1963:

> I was kind of eager and wide-eyed. Everything's so inchoate at that time, you're just *wanting*; there's some bleep calling. The *Kilkenny Magazine* was a wonderful thing for me because they did 'Mid-Term Break', which was written very quickly one evening in early February, when Christopher's anniversary was coming up. I sent it off and they took it almost by return of post. So that was a terrific sense of confirmation.

During this period, Heaney retained links with Queen's, and in particular with Alan Gabbey, now a lecturer in the Department of the History of Science, who edited a magazine called *Interest*, in which Heaney published some poems in 1962–3. It was Gabbey who first told Heaney about Philip Hobsbaum, a lecturer who had recently joined the English Department. Hobsbaum, who had read English under Leavis at Cambridge, was a poet himself and an admirer of Ted Hughes. He had organized regular sessions among poets, known as the 'Group', in London since the mid-1950s, in which poems by participants would be read and scrutinized. Heaney met him when he was beginning similar sessions in Belfast in the autumn of 1963, at about the time Heaney left schoolteaching and returned to St Joseph's as a lecturer in English. The meetings of the Belfast Group deepened the sense of confirmation Heaney had gained from his earliest publications. In the article 'The Group', written for the Belfast review, *The Honest Ulsterman*, in 1978, and reprinted in *Preoccupations*, Heaney describes Hobsbaum as 'one of the strongest agents of change' in a previously discouraging literary atmosphere:

> When Hobsbaum arrived in Belfast, he moved disparate elements into a single action. He emanated energy, generosity, belief in the community, trust in the parochial, the inept, the unprinted. He was impatient, dogmatic, relentlessly literary: yet he was patient with those he trusted, unpredictably susceptible to a wide variety of poems and personalities and urgent that the social and political exacerbations of our place should disrupt the decorums of literature.

The Group, which included, off and on, Michael Longley, Derek Mahon, Stewart Parker and James Simmons, met regularly in Hobsbaum's flat until he moved to Glasgow in 1966; and after that the sessions continued in Heaney's own house until 1970, attended in this later period by younger poets such as Paul Muldoon, Frank Ormsby and sometimes Michael Foley.

In addition to nurturing creative talent, Philip Hobsbaum was also a skilful entrepreneur, and he ensured that the work of the Group was brought to public attention. The poets were given some exposure in the Belfast Festival of 1965 which the journalist Mary Holland wrote up for the *Observer* in London, describing what she considered a cultural efflorescence in the city. The Festival produced a series of poetry pamphlets which, in addition to titles by Longley and Mahon, included, in November, Heaney's first small collection, *Eleven Poems*. Now, as then, Heaney resists any notion of a Belfast 'renaissance' in the mid-1960s, considering it 'a media event'. 'There was something there, but then there was something everywhere at that time: Liverpool, Newcastle – it was all the buoyancies.' It is certainly notable that when, in July 1966, he was given the opportunity to write at some length about Belfast in the 'Out of London' column in the *New Statesman*, he chose to use most of his space to analyse the deteriorating political situation and the ominous emergence of Ian Paisley, writing powerfully and resentfully for the Catholic position. Confining his description of the artistic scene to his concluding paragraphs, he nevertheless observed, with what optimism he could muster, that 'the possibility of a cultural life here is the possibility of salvation'.

By the time *Eleven Poems* was published, Heaney's own literary career was well under way. Hobsbaum had sent 'Groupsheets' to the poet and critic Edward Lucie-Smith, an associate from the days of the London Group, who forwarded them to various literary editors. Karl Miller of the *New Statesman* took three of Heaney's poems – 'Digging', 'Storm on the Island' and 'Scaffolding' – which he published together on 4 December 1964:

> Then inside six weeks or so I had a letter from Fabers. I just couldn't believe it, it was like getting a letter from God the Father. I had a collection of poems at that time with Dolmen Press in Dublin. I left it with them for about a month after I got the Faber letter and wrote and asked them had they taken any decision. I didn't say anything about Fabers, I felt that I could play *some* cards. Liam Miller sent the manuscript back to me and said they weren't quite sure. So I felt I acted honourably enough at Dolmen. If they'd said they were going to accept it, I might have been in a different position.

This was not, however, the manuscript which became *Death of a Naturalist*:

> Charles Monteith of Fabers asked me in January [1965] did I have a manuscript. I sent them what I had and they didn't think there was a book there but they would like first refusal if ever I thought I had a book. So in about

four months I wrote a hell of a lot, and I think I sent them another thing in about May or June. I got married in August and we went to London for our honeymoon, and by then they said they were going to take it. So it all happened very quickly.

Heaney had married Marie Devlin, whom he first met in October 1962. From a family of seven in Ardboe, Co. Tyrone, she had done a course in English and Speech and Drama at St Mary's College of Education in Belfast, and was teaching in intermediate school at the time of her marriage. The Heaneys had a son, Michael, in July 1966. Another son, Christopher, was born in February 1968, and a daughter, Catherine Ann, in April 1973.

In May 1966, when Heaney was 27, Fabers published his first full-length collection, *Death of a Naturalist*. It received, for a first volume, extraordinary critical acclaim. In England, Christopher Ricks in the *New Statesman* thought it 'outstanding'; C. B. Cox in the *Spectator* called it 'the best first book of poems I've read for some time', and Alan Ross in the *London Magazine* considered it 'a book of enormous promise'. In Ireland, John Hewitt in the *Belfast Telegraph* said that 'we confidently expect him to broaden his range and our imaginative estate'; Michael Longley in the *Irish Times* believed that 'his childhood landscape has acquired the validity of myth'; and the senior Irish poet Austin Clarke, reviewing it on Radio Eireann, said that 'unlike most first books, this one is mature and certain in its touch'. Heaney was given a Gregory Award for young writers, and subsequently *Death of a Naturalist* earned him the Somerset Maugham Award and the Geoffrey Faber Prize. These were the first of many major literary awards which Heaney has collected: they include the Denis Devlin Award (1973), the American-Irish Foundation Award (1973), the

W. H. Smith Prize (1975), the Duff Cooper Memorial Prize (1976), and the E. M. Forster Award (1976). This critical reception was obviously an enormous stimulus and encouragement to Heaney. It was also practically useful to him in being, no doubt, one of the factors which secured him a lectureship in English at Queen's when Philip Hobsbaum left for Glasgow in 1966.

In 1965 Heaney had begun to publish articles and reviews in various journals in England: he wrote an account of producing a mystery play in St Joseph's College, for instance, which he published in the teachers' journal, *The Use of English* ('A Chester Pageant', Autumn 1965), and he reviewed educational books for the *New Statesman*. In 1966 this kind of work broadened to include more comprehensive topical articles for the *New Statesman* and the *Listener*, and broadcasts for BBC radio and television: he became a fairly well-known communicator, on both cultural and political matters, in the late 1960s and early 1970s. This may be regarded, perhaps, as a translation into other areas of the educational career he had always imagined for himself, and it still persists in a more than usual accessibility for a poet held in high regard. His poetry readings, in particular, including the highly successful Faber poetry tour with Craig Raine in 1984, have kept him in the public eye.

In Heaney's first years as a lecturer at Queen's, the situation in Northern Ireland became more dangerous and tense, as the civil rights movement among Catholics gathered momentum and was met with fierce opposition from Protestant Loyalists and from the Royal Ulster Constabulary. On Saturday 5 October 1968, in Derry city, one of the most economically depressed areas even in Northern Ireland, the first major violent clash of the present 'Troubles' occurred when 2000 civil rights marchers, protesting mainly against gerrymandering (vote-rigging) and discriminatory housing allocations, defied a ban by the Home Affairs Minister, William Craig. Eighty-eight of them were injured in police baton charges, and television coverage of the march that evening was greeted with international outrage. Rioting followed in the Catholic Bogside area of Derry, and a few days later a large student protest march in Belfast city centre was organized from Queen's. Violence continued throughout Northern Ireland in the following months, and on 12 August 1969 there occurred the sectarian clashes in Derry which became known as the 'Battle of the Bogside'. On 14 August the British Army entered the city; and in January 1970 the Provisional IRA was officially formed in Dublin.

Heaney was himself involved in the civil rights movement, and after the 5 October 1968 march in Derry he wrote a piece in the *Listener*, 'Old Derry's Walls' (24 October 1968), on 'the indignation and determination of the civil rights marchers' and on Craig's 'bland indifference'. 'It seems now,' he said, 'that the Catholic minority, if it is to retain any self-respect, will have to risk the charge of wrecking the new moderation and seeking justice more vociferously'. The composer Sean O'Riada (for whom Heaney was later to write an elegy in *Field Work*) presented a programme on Radio Eireann and asked Heaney for a contribution. He provided the heavily ironical lyrics of a song called 'Craig's Dragoons', to be sung to the Loyalist tune, 'Dolly's Brae':

Come all ye Ulster loyalists and in full chorus join,
Think on the deeds of Craig's Dragoons who strike below
    the groin,
And drink a toast to the truncheon and the armoured
    water-hose
That mowed a swathe through Civil Rights and spat on
    Papish clothes.

We've gerrymandered Derry but Croppy won't lie down,
He calls himself a citizen and wants votes in the town.
But that Saturday in Duke Street we slipped the velvet
    glove –
The iron hand of Craig's Dragoons soon crunched a
    croppy dove. . . .

O William Craig, you are our love, our lily and our sash,
You have the boys who fear no noise, who'll batter and
    who'll bash.
They'll cordon and they'll baton-charge, they'll silence
    protest tunes,
They are the hounds of Ulster, boys, sweet William
    Craig's dragoons.

Heaney has only once since written such a directly
political song – a lamentation for the dead of Bloody
Sunday, 30 January 1972, when thirteen civilians
were killed by the British Army in Derry. Written for
the late Luke Kelly of the Dubliners folk group, it has
unfortunately never seen the light of day.

Heaney's second volume, *Door into the Dark*, was
published in June 1969. Although it was made a Choice
of the Poetry Book Society, a number of reviewers, while
appreciative, thought they sensed something tran-
sitional in the book – 'a formidable talent', as the poet
Norman Nicholson put it, 'biding his time before the
bigger gesture'. In the summer of 1969 Heaney was
actually in Madrid, visiting France and Spain on the
Somerset Maugham Award of the previous year: he
watched the events in the North on Spanish television,
as he remembers in 'Summer 1969' in the 'Singing
School' sequence of *North*. It was immediately clear to
him that the experience of 1969 must put its pressure
on his own work, as he explains in 'Feeling into Words'
in *Preoccupations*:

From that moment the problems of poetry moved from being simply a matter of achieving the satisfactory verbal icon to being a search for images and symbols adequate to our predicament. . . . I felt it imperative to discover a field of force in which . . . it would be possible to encompass the perspectives of a humane reason and at the same time to grant the religious intensity of the violence its deplorable authenticity and complexity.

When he read P. V. Glob's *The Bog People*, published in the same year, Heaney realized that his search for such 'images and symbols' had happened on one of its major discoveries. With its account of propitiatory Iron Age ritual killings in Jutland, and its extraordinarily compelling photographs of the bodies of the victims – preserved for two thousand years by the chemical properties of the peat bogs in which they had been buried – Glob's book seemed to offer an imaginative parallel for the Irish present. Heaney's meditation on it was eventually to produce his sequence of 'bog poems'.

He also, however, began to publish, in literary journals and reviews, some poems which addressed themselves more straightforwardly to the situation in the North – among them the poem 'Intimidation', which appeared in the Canadian journal *The Malahat Review* (no.17, 1970). It angrily bites out its resentment against the threatening Loyalist bonfires of the twelfth of July:

> Each year this reek
> Of their midsummer madness
> Troubles him, a nest of pismires
> At his drystone walls.
>
> Ghetto rats! Are they the ones
> To do the smoking out?
> They'll come streaming past
> To taste their ashes yet.

Several reviewers of Heaney's next collection, *Wintering Out*, of 1972, were disappointed that such poems as this did not appear in the book; and *North*, of 1975, which did reprint some of them (though not 'Intimidation'), was perhaps, at least in part, a response to these reviews. The more oblique strategy of the poems Heaney did collect in *Wintering Out* may be regarded, among other things, as an aspect of his response to the developing 'complexity' of the violence after the irruption into Northern affairs of the Provisional IRA in 1970, and particularly after the stepping up of their bombing campaign in 1971. After that, this kind of pugnacity would have been liable to misconstruction, to too casual an assimilation to positions with which Heaney would not be identified.

The academic year of 1970–1 was spent in America, at the University of California at Berkeley. Heaney read William Carlos Williams properly for the first time there, and later told James Randall that 'in the poems of *Wintering Out*, in the little quatrain shapes, there are signs of that loosening, the California spirit'. He also encountered the poetry of Gary Snyder, Robert Bly and Robert Duncan, and its engagement with protest against the war in Vietnam. He learnt from it a lesson he could apply to his own work in a different political context – the 'awareness', he told Randall, that poetry was 'a force, almost a mode of power, certainly a mode of resistance'. The year in America was also, however, 'a very Irish year too': Heaney got to know Tom Flanagan, the author of a book called *The Irish Novelists 1800–1850* (1959), and 'his concern with Irish history and literature, and his learning in it, were somehow fortifying, and gave me a conviction about the Irish theme, as it were'. Through Flanagan, Heaney also met Conor Cruise O'Brien, who was lecturing in the States that year. Heaney's poem 'Traditions', in *Wintering Out*, is dedicated to Flanagan; and Flanagan was later to publish his novel about 1798, *The Year of the French* (1979), in which, it has been said, the poet MacCarthy is partly based on Heaney.

Even in California, then, Heaney's mind was never far from Ireland: one of his pieces in the *Listener* that year noted grimly that 'while Berkeley shouts, Belfast burns'; and he began there a series of prose-poems which return once more to the world of his childhood in Co. Derry. Heaney did not complete the sequence in America, and was put off doing so by the appearance, in 1971, of Geoffrey Hill's volume of prose-poems, *Mercian Hymns*. 'What I had regarded as stolen marches in a form new to me had been headed off by a work of complete authority', he says in his preface to the eventual publication of the sequence, as a pamphlet called *Stations*, in Belfast in 1975, after he had completed it in May and June 1974. The sequence is of great interest, marking that vital moment in Heaney's career when, again as he has it in his preface, and as opposed to his first two books, 'the sectarian dimension of that pre-reflective experience presented itself as something asking to be uttered also'. It is a pity that it has never been given more permanent or more accessible publication.

When Heaney returned to Northern Ireland in September 1971, the situation had further deteriorated. Internment without trial had been introduced the previous month, and, as he wrote in the piece collected in *Preoccupations* as 'Christmas, 1971' – an article fraught with the anxiety, depression and tension of its moment – 'It hasn't been named martial law, but that's what it feels like'. By the time *Wintering Out* was published, however, in November 1972, Heaney had left the North for the Republic. He had resigned from his job at Queen's and moved, in August 1972, to a cottage at Glanmore, near Ashford, a very beautiful, secluded area in Co. Wicklow, about twenty miles from Dublin, where he began to work as a freelance writer.

Heaney has offered various explanations of the move, and it seems clear that there were artistic, practical and political reasons for it. Afraid of becoming locked into familiar patterns of working in Belfast, he wanted, as he says in the foreword to *Preoccupations*, 'to put the practice of poetry more deliberately at the centre of my life. It was a kind of test.' In practical terms, he had been offered the Glanmore cottage at an extremely low rent by the Canadian academic, Ann Saddlemeyer; this, together with the fact that in the Republic writers' incomes are untaxed, was obviously an attraction for a man with a family giving up a salaried job. But the move also, as Heaney of course realized, had an 'emblematic' significance. It was read as a decisive political alignment: literally *read*, since Ian Paisley's paper, the *Protestant Telegraph*, bade farewell to 'the well-known papist propagandist' on his return to 'his spiritual home in the popish republic', and the *Irish Times* in Dublin welcomed him with an editorial headlined 'Ulster Poet Moves South'. Heaney's most revealing interpretation of the 'emblem' of his move occurs in an interview with his close friend Seamus Deane in the *New York Times Book Review* in 1979, where he offers his opinion that, whereas for the Northern Protestant writer, the Troubles could be regarded as a mere 'interruption' of the status quo,

> For the Catholic writer, I think the Troubles were a critical moment, a turning point, possibly a vision of some kind of fulfilment. The blueprint in the Catholic writer's head predicted that a history would fulfil itself

[31]

in a United Ireland or in something. . . . In the late
'60s and early '70s the world was changing for the
Catholic imagination. I felt I was compromising
some part of myself by staying in a situation where
socially and, indeed, imaginatively, there were pressures
'against' regarding the moment as critical. Going to the
South was perhaps emblematic for me and was certainly
so for some of the people I knew. To the Unionists it looked
like a betrayal of the Northern thing.

The move nevertheless inevitably occasioned anxieties
– about missing a major historical moment; about
being thought, in some way, to have abandoned a
responsibility. Such self-doubt, together with the
media attention the move received, fuels one of Heaney's
finest poems, 'Exposure'.

In Glanmore Heaney immediately set to work on a
version of the long medieval Irish poem, *Buile Suibhne*
(literally, *The Madness of Sweeney*):

I was going to be free and I wanted to make sure
I had tasks to fill my life. I was thinking of myself
as a professional writer for the first time, and I thought
of it as a kind of freelance writer's enterprise, among
other things: I had a half-notion that I might get
a children's story out of it, and a radio programme.
I'd spoken to an actor, Jacky MacGowran, a wonderful
man, whom I thought of as a Sweeney, perhaps, and
he expressed an interest. Then when he died in 1973
a little bit of the steam went out of it for me.
But the prose sections were written with the notion
of a radio link, almost: that's why they were
chastened down from their rather euphuistic shape in
the original.

A first version of the whole thing was completed very
quickly, by April 1973, done with 'a strong sense of
bending the text to my purposes' (St Ronan, for in-
stance, was referred to as 'the bully boy', when the

Unionists were accused of using 'bully boy tactics' in the North; and Sweeney was given such lines as 'My relief was a pivot of history'). Deciding that this version was too 'infected with the idiom of the moment', Heaney put it aside for as long as seven years (apart from the section he called 'Sweeney Praises the Trees', which he recited occasionally at readings). Then, after a semester in Harvard in 1979, he 'just jumped on it' again while staying with his family in a house on Long Island lent to him by Tom Flanagan. This time he knew he wanted it to be 'bare and fairly obedient and plain and strict in some way'; and, returning to Ireland, he completed it over the next year or so and first published it, as *Sweeney Astray*, in 1983.

It is hardly surprising that the first version was so attuned to the contemporary moment, since Heaney was working simultaneously on those poems of his which most directly confront Northern sectarianism, the poems of *North* itself, which eventually appeared in June 1975. Keeping the promise made in the opening line of 'The Tollund Man', he had in fact visited Aarhus, in Denmark, in October 1973, and had seen in the museum there the preserved bodies described in *The Bog People*. Heaney's growing belief in the relevance and usefulness of this material to his own work was confirmed when Ted Hughes enthusiastically greeted the earliest bog poems and encouraged him to go on with them. Hughes's sister, Olwyn, published a limited edition of the whole series, as *Bog Poems*, from her Rainbow Press in 1975.

The archaeologizing appetite of Heaney's imagination was also being fed at this time by events in Dublin itself:

Irish archaeology was on the move in the late sixties and early seventies. When I came down here there were excavations going on, and the revisionism about the Vikings was in the air. I had a sympathetic interest in it

[33]

– not very systematically reading up on it, but I knew Tom Delaney [the archaeologist, now dead, recalled in 'Station Island VIII'] and through him I got some little flicker of intimacy with it. I remember going to the *Viking Dublin* exhibition in the National Museum and seeing the child's drawing and the combs, the little scale-pans and so on. I was terrifically awakened to all that Bronze Age stuff; I used to love the gold. It was just that my receiving stations were open for it for a couple of years.

It was during this period too that Heaney began, or deepened, his study of three poets who have profoundly affected his subsequent work: Yeats, the modern Russian poet Osip Mandelstam, and Dante.

North was greeted with great critical acclaim in the English press, most reviewers delighted that Northern Ireland had finally found what they considered appropriate expression in poetry. Martin Dodsworth's review in the *Guardian*, which declared the book 'unequalled in our contemporary poetry as a testimony to the patience, persistence and power of the imagination under duress', may be considered representative, if more hyperbolic than some. Of particular note was Conor Cruise O'Brien's account in the *Listener*: 'I had the uncanny feeling, reading these poems,' he wrote, 'of listening to the thing itself, the actual substance of historical agony and dissolution, the tragedy of a people in a place: the Catholics of Northern Ireland'. The book's reception in Northern Ireland itself was less warm: in *The Honest Ulsterman* Ciaran Carson castigated Heaney as 'the laureate of violence – a mythmaker, an anthropologist of ritual killing', and Edna Longley thought that 'a poet who has already articulated so much of the experience of his people and country in oblique terms has no need to prove his credentials'.

In a 'Books of the Year' column for the *Observer* the

Christmas after *North* was published, however, the greatly admired American poet Robert Lowell described it as 'a new kind of political poetry by the best Irish poet since W. B. Yeats'. When Heaney was awarded the Duff Cooper Memorial Prize for the volume the following year, it was Lowell who presented it to him. Many critics have discerned the influence of Lowell on Heaney's work, particularly on the poems in his next book, *Field Work*, of 1979, which included an elegy for Lowell, who died in 1977. Heaney also gave the address at his memorial service in London, and clearly the relationship, though brief, was an important one for him:

The first time I met him was in 1972 in London. The night he got married to Caroline [Blackwood], there was a party in Sonia Orwell's, and Karl Miller, whom I was staying with, took me over to it. We talked a bit then, but I was extremely shy of him, because he had this aura of a great classic: when I was an undergraduate we were reading 'The Quaker Graveyard' in that old Geoffrey Moore anthology of American poetry. Then when *History* and *For Lizzie and Harriet* and *The Dolphin* came out together in 1973 I did a thing on *Imprint* on the radio, and he got a copy of it and wrote and thanked me. I never thought much about it, but later I wrote and asked him would he do a reading in Kilkenny [at an arts festival Heaney was involved in there in 1975]. He spent a week in Kilkenny and stayed on afterwards and came to see us in Wicklow. That was a wonderful, happy time. Then he used to come here with Caroline; they had a flat out in the big house, Castletown, and we went out for meals and so on. I find that in the matter of relationships with writers and confirmations from writers, it's not necessary always to talk about poetry; it's a sensation that you have, and an instinct you have, that the other person regards you somehow, and that's a kind of fortification of your own confidence. In a sense, that's more important than any technical thing that can be said. I felt I got that from Lowell a bit. But I must also say that when I read those *Lizzie and Harriet* books, I loved the ignorance, I loved the destruction he had practised upon the lyric. It may have been an error in the end but, at that particular moment, the bull-headedness, the rage and uncharmingness of the writing attracted me enormously. I mean, it *may* have been an error, but there was some kind of morality about it, I thought. But I love *Near the Ocean* too, those Marvellian stanzas; I think that 'Waking Early Sunday Morning' is a terrific poem, it's a great, public, noble piece of work. And then *Life Studies* is a kind of necessary book, you know, it's *the* book, in some ways.

The radio programme Heaney refers to there, *Imprint*, was one he hosted himself on Radio Eireann on and off from 1973 to 1977, at first fortnightly and later weekly. This was done 'as journeywork, to make money'; but he came to feel, by 1975, for domestic and practical reasons, that he would have to return to a full-time job in order to buy a house in Dublin itself. He started as a full-time member of the English Department at a teachers' training college in Dublin, Carysfort, in October 1975, and the family eventually moved into Dublin in November 1976, to the Edwardian house in Sandymount which they still occupy. Heaney was made head of the department in Carysfort in 1976, and stayed in that post until 1981. He now regards the decision to take the original job as, in some ways, a 'caving-in':

I felt there was something terrifically enabling and freeing about the risks and exposure of living in Wicklow in that way, and you had to prove yourself. In order to prove yourself, you had to feel you had achieved something in your art, that you had verified your life. Somehow when you get onto the cushions of a salaried position, that neediness and sense of danger disappears. It's a different

kind of engagement with the world, of course, but I'm
ever grateful for that little moment of 'exposure'.

What he did initially like about the job, however – its
offering him a less public role than he felt he would
have had in a university in the Republic, 'a little lean-
to that would shelter me with a salary and leave me
alone' – came to have its drawbacks too. In addition to
feeling himself 'crumbling down into an administrator
again', the Irish Catholic forms and presuppositions of
such an institution seemed to be demanding from him
a degree of ratification which he felt increasingly un-
able to give.

From the early 1970s on, Heaney's reputation had
been growing in America and, in 1979, the year he
published his fifth volume, *Field Work* – a book whose
character derives largely from his 'pastoral' years in
Glanmore – he had spent a term in Harvard as one of
several temporary successors to Robert Lowell, who
had taught a poetry workshop there. At the end of
1980, he was offered a five-year contract by Harvard,
to teach there for one term a year; and, having decided
in 1981 to resign from his job at Carysfort, he started
at Harvard in January 1982. In 1984 he was elected to
the Boylston Chair of Rhetoric and Oratory there, a
chair first held by John Quincy Adams, and always
subsequently kept for writers. Since he began teaching
at Harvard, Heaney has divided his time between
America and Dublin, spending four months every year
in Harvard, where he conducts two poetry workshops
with students he has himself selected:

> It's the sort of thing that went on in the Group in Belfast,
> except that it's a bit more ritualized, and the system
> permits it in America. It's actually quite exhausting,
> because you are like the centre of a target, and there are
> twenty-eight human arrows coming at you all the time,
> flighted with manuscripts, and each time you meet one

of them there's a judgement to be made, and there's a *tactful* judgement to be made.

Heaney is delighted with, and grateful for, the audience his work has attracted in the States, but still surprised by it:

Their noise isn't my noise, their concerns aren't my concerns. Luckily, the English language and the art of verse sometimes link us but I'm puzzled, in a way, that they can actually *read* some of the stuff. It's the texture and the inner dynamics of a poem that interest them, and of course poems have to be able to live in that way. My impatience with a lot of American poetry is that that's the *only* way it can live. In one way, of course, that's all there is: there's just a form, and there's a form housing a set of harmonies and balances. But I think that in the culture and situation I come from, you want to punish the form with some relationship to the actual. It seems to me that in a lot of contemporary American poetry the words have less specific gravity than they have within the language in Ireland and Britain. They are on a kind of bouncy moonwalk, the language just *floats*. There's a kind of wafting garrulousness about it. Our difficulty here is something opposite; it's a kind of cross-legged, prim-mouthed thing.

Much as Heaney admires, then, some American poets who are more or less his contemporaries – Robert Pinsky, Robert Hass and Frank Bidart, for instance – he feels most affinity, in the States, with three expatriate poets who also teach and write there: Derek Walcott from the Caribbean; Joseph Brodsky from Russia; and Czeslaw Milosz from Poland (whose prose work *Native Realm* is quoted in the poem 'Away from it All' in *Station Island*):

Walcott didn't divest himself of what are, in one way, the marks of the conqueror, in another way the resources of English tradition. His negotiation between poles, the exterior pole of literature, London and the world out there, and the inner pole of the Caribbean – it kind of interested me, that balance. I first met Brodsky at the time when I had just started out in Wicklow, and I liked his sense of exile and his intensity – someone *absolutely* a poet, you know. The three of us have a language which involves *English* literature, in a way, and involves a different sense of the world of literature from most American poetry. Milosz I just find enormously close: the wonderful sense of loss of what is most cherished, and the way he can turn what, in lesser hands or with a lesser writer, would be a poem of personal nostalgia into a symptom of great cultural and historical change, without portentousness. That move from personal lyric lament to visionary, tragic lamentation: I just love the *note*. And he's so stern too, he's both stern and tender, and I like that very much. And I guess somewhere in it all is a closeness because of the kind of Catholic subculture into which his sensibility pays, and out of which it springs. It's not a note that you hear in English language poetry very much because, both in America and in England, the religious sensibility has been bred out of the poetry.

1980 was a stocktaking year for Heaney, with the simultaneous publication of his *Selected Poems* and his collection of prose pieces, *Preoccupations*, in October. In 1982 he co-edited with Ted Hughes a poetry anthology for older children, *The Rattle Bag* (which includes his own delightful translation of a Middle English poem, 'The Names of the Hare'), and in 1983 he published *Sweeney Astray* in Ireland. It was published in England simultaneously with *Station Island* in October 1984.

The decision to publish *Sweeney Astray* in Ireland first was made as the result of Heaney's present major public commitment there, his directorship, along with several others, including Tom Paulin and Seamus Deane, of the Field Day company. This was initially a theatre company formed in Derry in 1980 by Heaney's close friend, the playwright Brian Friel, and the actor Stephen Rea, to produce Friel's play *Translations* outside the commercial theatre. The play, set in 1833, locates a crucial moment in the death of the Irish language, making of it an implicit parable for the Irish present. Its examination of Irish history, and its directed effort to address the relationship between Ireland and England, thereby attempting to combat the stasis and apathy of the North, may be seen as the essential signatures of Field Day. It is certainly in this context that Heaney viewed the initial publication of *Sweeney Astray*:

> The act of publishing is a sign, a gesture, a form of solidarity; and I always thought that when *Sweeney* came out I would publish it in Ireland. When we started Field Day, I liked the idea of it being published in Derry. It's a kind of all-Ireland event situated just within the North, and there's a little bit of submerged political naughtiness in that. This was one of the reasons I translated the placenames into their modern equivalents: I hoped that gradually the Northern Unionist or Northern Protestant readership might, in some minuscule way, feel free to identify with the Gaelic tradition.

Heaney's other personal venture with Field Day so far has been the publication in 1983 of a fairly lengthy pamphlet poem, *An Open Letter*. This received a lot of media attention, since in it he dissociated himself from the adjective 'British' under which he was classified by the editors of the *Penguin Book of Contemporary British Poetry* in 1982:

> Caesar's Britain, its *partes tres*,
> United England, Scotland, Wales,
> *Britannia* in the old tales,
>   Is common ground.

> *Hibernia* is where the Gaels
>   Made a last stand
>
> And long ago were stood upon –
> End of simple history lesson.
> As empire rings its curtain down
>   This 'British' word
> Sticks deep in native and *colon*
>   Like Arthur's sword.

Heaney's own doubts about the advisability of publishing that poem – he now wishes that he had addressed himself to the issue of 'British' literature more fully in prose – are one measure of his present hesitation between declaration and withdrawal:

> I advance and retire from any conscious or deliberate entry into that public life. I've got so much attention that my impulse is to retreat rather than to go forward at this stage. I don't know whether that's an irresponsibility or a salutary piece of survival. I just don't know; these are questions that I'm not too clear about myself.

The 'attention' is not in any doubt: Seamus Heaney is an enormously popular poet (most of his volumes have sold well into five figures, a staggering number for a contemporary poet); Queen's University awarded him the honorary degree of Doctor of Literature in 1982, and there have been others, including one from the Open University in 1984; his critical reputation is assured, and growing; and his exemplary status in contemporary Irish cultural life is witnessed by the way the best commentators (in, for instance, the influential journal *The Crane Bag*) constantly adduce his work as a point of reference. He has indeed been what he has one of his characters in 'Station Island' call him, a 'poet, lucky poet'.

It is significant, however, that that remark is made

in a context which turns recognition into something very like rebuke; and the self-accusations of his later work define an uncomplacent refusal to stay still, to rest secure in any fixed position – particularly, perhaps, the fixed position of his own reputation. If being 'in between' was a *donnée* of his birth, his exemplary quality derives from his disciplined, resourceful and subtle negotiation of boundaries which he has chosen, as well as been chosen by; and his work may be admiringly characterized in the terms of approbation he has himself offered others (in his preface to a collection of pieces from *The Crane Bag*): it is inscribed with 'the good force of creative mind at work in the light of conscience'.

II

Roots and Reading:
Death of a Naturalist (1966) and *Door into the Dark* (1969)

> I began as a poet when my roots were crossed with my reading.
>
> Seamus Heaney, 'Feeling into Words'

Seamus Heaney's first two books derive their primary material from his own first world, his rural childhood and young manhood in Co. Derry; and, although this world maintains a presence in every one of Heaney's subsequent volumes, *Death of a Naturalist* and *Door into the Dark* explore and exhaust a particular way of treating it. *Door into the Dark*, however, is also a transitional book which, if it contains poems that would not have been out of place in the first book, also points forward to *Wintering Out*. It seems appropriate, then, to consider both volumes together under the general rubric of the 'early work', but to hold them apart too, initially, in an attempt to describe the individual character of each.

Death of a Naturalist

What its original reviewers singled out for praise in Heaney's first volume is still, perhaps, its most obvious feature: the observed and recollected facts of his early rural experience are conveyed in a language of great sensuous richness and directness. Digging potatoes and turf, picking blackberries, shooting, churning butter and ploughing are all rendered in poems which, like the synaesthetic blur of the bluebottles in 'Death

[43]

of a Naturalist' itself, weave 'a strong gauze of sound' around their occasions. The most obvious character- istics of this sound are its onomatopoeia and its alliter- ative effects. The onomatopoeia – 'the squelch and slap / Of soggy peat' in 'Digging', 'the plash and gurgle of the sour-breathed milk, / the pat and slap of small spades on wet lumps' in 'Churning Day' – is the element in Heaney's work which most readily lends itself to parody: Philip Hobsbaum (in Curtis, ed., *The Art of Seamus Heaney*, p. 37) has described it as 'Heaneyspeak . . . the snap-crackle-and-pop of diction'. It can also, however, produce such extraordinary effects as the 'bass chorus' of the frogs in 'Death of a Naturalist':

> Right down the dam gross-bellied frogs were cocked
> On sods; their loose necks pulsed like sails. Some hopped:
> The slap and plop were obscene threats. Some sat
> Poised like mud grenades, their blunt heads farting.

The sheer noise Heaney manages to make out of English vowels there is remarkable – a dissonant cacophony that forces the mouth to work overtime if the reader speaks the lines aloud. Some of the alliterative effects of the poems are equally striking: the clamour and clang of the opening line of 'Churning Day', for in- stance – 'A thick crust, coarse-grained as limestone rough-cast' or, in 'Blackberry-Picking', 'We hoarded the fresh berries in the byre. / But when the bath was filled we found a fur . . . ,' the second line of which imitates the alliterative line of Anglo-Saxon poetry, with its four main stresses, three carrying the heavy alliteration.

Such effects came naturally enough to Heaney, no doubt, as the result of his interest in Anglo-Saxon poetry and in Hopkins; but, sanctioned by Ted Hughes's absorption of similar early influences, they seemed to ally him, in 1966, with a reaction against some of the decorums of recent English poetry. Almost expecting the epithet 'earthy' ('his words give us the soil-reek of Ireland, the colourful violence of his childhood on a farm in Derry', said C. B. Cox in his *Spectator* review), his poems seemed designed to go where A. Alvarez said English poetry should go in his introduction to *The New Poetry*, the famous Penguin anthology of 1962, 'beyond the gentility principle'. (This is not without its ironies, since Alvarez has been Heaney's most severe critic.)

That anthology singled out Ted Hughes for praise; and some of Hughes's stylistic devices are obviously a direct, indeed an overwhelming, influence, on some of the poems of *Death of a Naturalist*: on the trick of eliding title into first line in 'The Diviner' and 'Trout'; on the almost absurd range of military metaphors in 'Trout' itself and in 'Cow in Calf'; and on the similar metaphors and portentously over-insistent anthropomorphisms in 'Turkeys Observed' ('He lorded it on the claw-flecked mud / With a grey flick of his Confucian eye'). These poems have their eyes so eagerly trained on *The Hawk in the Rain* and *Lupercal*, Hughes's first two books, that trout and cow and turkeys disappear unrecognizably into pale imitation and pastiche.

It is possible to feel, however, that something more subtle and complex has been learnt from Hughes in 'Digging', where the shape and movement of Hughes's well-known 'The Thought-Fox' seems to have been deeply assimilated and absorbed. Although the ostensible subject matter of the poems is quite different, both situate their poets behind a window, pen in hand, in the act of composition. The Hughes poem is more specifically preoccupied with its own making, as it intently conjures up the notion and image of 'fox' which – a 'thought' made word – is also the conjuration of the poem itself. 'The Thought-Fox' conveys an impression of utter concentration, as what is recollected from experience stirs again in the 'darkness' of creative imagination, and issues eventually in the words which recreate that life on the page:

> Till, with a sudden sharp hot stink of fox
> It enters the dark hole of the head.
> The window is starless still; the clock ticks,
> The page is printed.

Heaney's poem is less intent on its own process and more concerned, ultimately, to enforce a moral and propound an aesthetic, but its progress is very similar to Hughes's. The sight of his father digging below the window conjures a memory of him digging potatoes 'twenty years away' and, beyond that, of his grand-father digging turf; and just as the fox enters 'the dark hole of the head' in 'The Thought-Fox', these associated memories merge in Heaney's head, and emerge as words on the page:

> The cold smell of potato mould, the squelch and slap
> Of soggy peat, the curt cuts of an edge
> Through living roots awaken in my head.
> But I've no spade to follow men like them.
>
> Between my finger and my thumb
> The squat pen rests.
> I'll dig with it.

The pen–spade analogy is, of course, the major point of the poem, and it is characteristically Heaney's own, as I shall suggest in a moment; but the poem's shape, and its self-consciousness about the relationship between exterior and interior, experience and language, nature and mind, show Heaney inheriting something much richer and more sustaining in early Hughes than the tics and tricks of subservient reflex pastiche. The way in which Heaney makes the inherited shape his own in 'Digging' is a very early indication of his true strength: he is not subdued to, but liberated by, the achievement of his earliest exemplar.

Although it is possible to detect a variety of relatively unabsorbed influences on Heaney's first poems – Robert Frost, Robert Graves and Norman MacCaig, for instance – I think a similar liberation may be discovered in what *Death of a Naturalist* absorbs from Patrick Kavanagh and from Wordsworth. There is no formal indebtedness to Kavanagh in the book – the chanciness, unpredictability and *sui generis* nature of his work make him inimitable – although 'At a Potato Digging' may have been sanctioned, at some level, by 'The Great Hunger', Kavanagh's long poem on the metaphorical 'hunger' (for a more fulfilling existence) of the small Co. Monaghan farmer, which opens by watching 'the potato-gatherers like mechanized scare-crows move / Along the sidefall of the hill'. Nevertheless, the presumption made by Kavanagh that such hidden Irish rural experience was a proper subject for poetry in English was genuinely liberating for Heaney, who is on record as saying that 'I have no need to write a poem to Patrick Kavanagh: I wrote *Death of a Naturalist*' (quoted in Dunn, ed., *Two Decades of Irish Writing*, p. 35).

Some of the central poems in the book, however, maintain a major allegiance to Wordsworth. 'Death of a Naturalist' itself, 'The Barn' and 'Blackberry-Picking' are, as it were, written in the margin of such passages as the boat-stealing episode in Book 1 of *The Prelude*, and the separate poem 'Nutting' (originally intended for *The Prelude*), both of which Heaney and Hughes include in *The Rattle Bag* anthology. These are poems in which an enlargement of consciousness is enacted in some interchange between mind and nature. In the passage from *The Prelude*, the stealing of the boat – 'an act of stealth / And troubled pleasure' – is repaid by the child's terror of a huge cliff which, 'As if with voluntary power instinct', seems to stride after him, leaving its aftertaste in his imagination when

> . . . huge and mighty forms, that do not live
> Like living men, moved slowly through my mind
> By day, and were the trouble of my dreams.

In 'Nutting', the child's act of hostility towards nature – the wanton destruction of a hazel copse – is succeeded by guilt and remorse:

> unless I now
> Confound my present feelings with the past,
> Even then, when from the bower I turned away
> Exulting, rich beyond the wealth of kings,
> I felt a sense of pain when I beheld
> The silent trees and the intruding sky.

These moments in Wordsworth are part of the process of Nature's education of the poet, moments in which the child's knowledge of reality is extended. In Heaney, 'The Barn' enforces a similar knowledge when it moves, towards its close, 'Over the rafters of sleep', into a nightmarishly specific instance of 'huge and mighty forms': 'I lay face-down to shun the fear above. / The two-lugged sacks moved in like great blind rats.' Both 'Death of a Naturalist' and 'Blackberry-Picking' come to an end with explicit statements of the new knowledge acquired during the incidents they describe. At the end of 'Death of a Naturalist', after seeing the 'angry frogs' which can develop out of jars of frogspawn, and hearing their bass chorus, 'I sickened, turned and ran. The great slime kings / Were gathered there for vengeance and I knew / That if I dipped my hand the spawn would clutch it.' The reaction is exactly that of the child in *The Prelude* – 'With trembling hands I turned'; and Heaney's 'I knew' is the terrified knowledge of the threat implicit in apparently benign natural forms. The guilty fantasy of the frogs' 'vengeance' for his act of seizing frogspawn is prefigured by Wordsworth's fantasy of being hounded by the cliff.

At the end of 'Blackberry-Picking', the knowledge comes not in fantasy but in the forced acknowledgement of actuality when the picked blackberries ferment: 'I always felt like crying. It wasn't fair / That all the lovely canfuls smelt of rot. / Each year I hoped they'd keep, knew they would not.' 'It wasn't fair' is the child's querulous, petulant recognition of inevitability, the stamped foot with which he responds to a world which will never measure his desires; and this knowledge, as the poem's metaphorical language intimates, is also heavy with the knowledge of sexuality: the first blackberry's 'flesh was sweet', leaving 'lust for / Picking', and the children's palms end up 'sticky as Bluebeard's' (the murderer of numerous wives in Perrault's famous tale). The sexual metaphor is also present in 'Nutting', where the hazel copse is 'A virgin scene' in which the child 'with wise restraint, / Voluptuous, fearless of a rival, eyed / The banquet' before shattering it with 'merciless ravage', a kind of rape leaving the copse 'Deformed and sullied'. In both Wordsworth and Heaney, the sexual implication is developed naturally out of the anecdote: both 'Nutting' and 'Blackberry-Picking' are poems about the end of innocence.

The 'death of a naturalist' is also, however, the birth of a poet; and what seems now of most interest in this first book of Heaney's is the relationship in it between his early experience and his early experience of writing poetry. The trying on of different styles and manners, the rhyming of his own experiences with poems by Hughes, Kavanagh and Wordsworth, in the aim of discovering his own individual voice and note, is a matter of eager enjoyment in *Death of a Naturalist*, a relished sounding of what he has called the 'echo-chamber' of the head, in order to learn his own capacity. This exuberant performance of the present moment of the poem is the essential signature of the book, and it frequently protects it from the commonest emotion in poems which recollect childhood experience, nostalgia. The poems are so clearly delighted that the early experience has provided their own inspiration that the pastness or lostness of the experience itself is dissolved in the joy of creativity.

This joy, however, derives also from Heaney's view of his own poetry as, in certain important respects, continuous with the rural experience it describes: hence those poems in which he discovers, in his first world, analogies for the art of poetry, 'The Diviner' and 'Digging' itself. When he discusses 'The Diviner' in 'Feeling into Words', Heaney points up the analogy quite straightforwardly, telling us that Philip Sidney in his *Apology for Poetry* refers to the Latin *vates* for 'poet', 'which is as much as a Diviner': both poet and diviner seem, to Heaney, to have 'a gift for mediating between the latent resource and the community that wants it current and released'. The point of the analogy, therefore, is to enforce the notion of the poet as intimately involved with his own community, serving it with words as the diviner serves it with water. It is interesting that the poem itself, however, discovers its central metaphor not in the primary world of the diviner, or in the secondary world of the poet, but in a tertiary realm, that of radio: 'The rod jerked down with precise convulsions, / Spring water suddenly broadcasting / Through a green aerial its secret stations.' The metaphor is entirely apt in the way it imagines both poet and diviner seizing out of the air an otherwise invisible, or inaudible, reality; and it is also apt in that it reminds us how a culture has developed from, and is still rooted in, an agriculture, since to 'broadcast' was originally to cast seed widely over the land. The careful aptness of the metaphor, alert to etymology, is in keeping with the poem's own care to give the diviner his due, and not merely to appropriate him as an analogy: there is no forcing of similitude, and nothing in the poem asserts it. It is insinuated, not insisted.

I am not at all sure that the same can be said for the better-known 'Digging'. The basic metaphor – the pen as spade – informs a great deal of Heaney's subsequent work, when it is translated out of its specifically agricultural application into a view of poetry as archaeology, the poem as an act of cultural and historical retrieval. In 'Digging', the poem confesses the discontinuity between spade and pen before it asserts a willed continuity:

> But I've no spade to follow men like them.
>
> Between my finger and my thumb
> The squat pen rests.
> I'll dig with it.

In 'Feeling into Words', Heaney speaks of this poem as if it is an illustration of the 'proverbial' wisdom of a saying remembered from his childhood, 'the pen's lighter than the spade'. In fact, however, this is the wisdom of an agricultural labourer who knows the heaviness of the spade, and knows that there is something easier as a way of life: the word 'lighter' in the saying opens a huge gap between the worlds of manual work and education. That gap is narrowed in 'Digging' to the single blank line before its final stanza; and the analogy, far from acknowledging the pen's lightness, in fact wants to make it 'squat' and heavy again. The strain of over-determination in this shows up in what Heaney has himself called the 'theatricality' of the poem's opening lines, where the pen is not only spade but gun – which is at least one analogy too many for a short poem; and it shows too in the false note of the backslapping exclamation, 'By God, the old man could handle a spade', which may register genuine filial pride but which, in a poem rather than a conversation, sounds as if it is trying too hard: what should be all casual ease in fact sounds quite uneasy.

Nevertheless, if the poem is over-assertive in the enforcing of its moral, and in the proposing of a first aesthetic – thereby betraying, despite itself, an insecurity – it is also an extremely important poem in the Heaney *œuvre*, in that it opens up, as soon as the work itself opens up, an issue which remains at the root of a large number of subsequent poems – the proper relationship between this poet and his own first community. As 'Digging' indicates, this is primarily, in *Death of a Naturalist*, the relationship with his immediate family – father and grandfather in 'Digging', his father alone in a number of other poems, his younger brother's death in 'Mid-Term Break', his mother glimpsed in 'Churning Day', his father's uncle in 'Ancestral Photograph'. These are all affectionate family memories, registering intimacy, warmth, tenderly respectful recall. But 'Follower', another poem of recollection, makes a more resigned admission of the gap between first and second worlds, with its contrast between 'now' and 'then' and the sudden move towards its close which reverses the paternal and filial roles:

> I wanted to grow up and plough,
> To close one eye, stiffen my arm.
> All I ever did was follow
> In his broad shadow round the farm.

I was a nuisance, tripping, falling,
Yapping always. But today
It is my father who keeps stumbling
Behind me, and will not go away.

When the artist Noel Connor accompanied this poem
with a drawing for the collection *Gravities* in 1979, he
drew a large dark bird, its wings spread in flight, dimly
visible behind a spider's web opening and spreading
towards the viewer; and this quasi-Joycean imagery
appropriately counterpoints the poem's own sense of
being constricted by one's entanglement in family and
first world. The irritation and impatience of its con-
clusion are, perhaps, a measure of how the 'father' in
'Follower' is, as well as being the actual biological
father, that network of loyalties and attachments
which can be as much confinement as consolation in
any first world. 'Follower' is the clearest instance in
Death of a Naturalist of what Heaney later describes in
Patrick Kavanagh as 'the penalty of consciousness, the
unease generated when a milieu becomes material'
('From Monaghan to the Grand Canal' in *Preoccupations*).

In the poem which closes the book, 'Personal
Helicon', there are signs that this kind of self-
consciousness is eventually to become a more openly
admitted element in the work. The poem, about
Heaney's own poetry, is dedicated to his fellow Nor-
thern Irish poet, Michael Longley, and it owes some-
thing to the greenhouse poems of Theodore Roethke
(on whom Heaney writes in *Preoccupations*), which
similarly elaborate a psychology from a symbolically
suggestive childhood world of vegetal process. In
'Personal Helicon', unlike 'The Diviner' and 'Digging',
that world does not provide analogies for poetry, but it
is itself turned into a little myth of poetic inspiration:
the wells and springs of Heaney's childhood become the

[53]

springs of the Muses' mountain of Helicon, which were sources of inspiration for anyone who drank there. In the personal myth of the poem, Helicon is crossed with Narcissus, who fell in love with his own reflection; and the images of inspiration derived from the childhood world are images of circularity and reflexivity – the wells 'had echoes, gave back your own call / With a clean new music in it'. When, at the end of the poem, Heaney articulates an aim for his own work – 'I rhyme / To see myself, to set the darkness echoing' – it is to emphasize the possibly narcissistic self-entrancement of poetry. If 'Digging' and 'The Diviner' humbly make the poet the inheritor of rural traditions of labour and service, 'Personal Helicon' more egotistically suggests that the importance of the poem lies in its ability to reveal the poet to himself, restoring in language what has been lost in reality. Established in *Death of a Naturalist*, these are the poles of social responsibility and of self-exploration between which all of Heaney's subsequent work has oscillated.

Door into the Dark

The title of Heaney's second collection obviously links the book to the final lines of *Death of a Naturalist*, implying a renewed attempt, in poetry, 'To see myself, to set the darkness echoing'; and the link is further emphasized in the *Selected Poems* where, having concluded the selection from *Death of a Naturalist* with 'Personal Helicon', Heaney opens the *Door into the Dark* poems with 'The Forge', whose first line provides his new title – 'All I know is a door into the dark'. The word 'dark' does indeed echo throughout the second book, perhaps so frequently as to seem a little over-intended and programmatic. The darkness of the self suggested by 'Personal Helicon' is, however, only one of the 'darks' to which the book's door gives access: the others are those of artistic creation itself and, increasingly towards the book's close, of the Irish landscape and its history.

When he discusses his title in 'Feeling into Words', Heaney says that he intended it to 'gesture towards' the idea of poetry as 'a point of entry into the buried life of the feelings or as a point of exit for it. Words themselves are doors; Janus is to a certain extent their deity, looking back to a ramification of roots and associations and forward to a clarification of sense and meaning.' This has its consonance with T. S. Eliot's well-known concept of the 'dark embryo' within the poet 'which gradually takes on the form and speech of a poem'; and *Door into the Dark* does have its actual embryos and foetuses – in 'Mother', 'Cana Revisited' and 'Elegy for a Still-Born Child'. I think it is possible to regard it as a book in which a new, finer and more subtle kind of Heaney poem seems to be embryonically present, but not yet quite born. If Heaney has himself defined one way in which Janus is its appropriate god, I would suggest another: some of its poems, particularly the analogy poems, 'The Forge' and 'Thatcher', look back to one of the major kinds in *Death of a Naturalist*, whereas others, and in particular the concluding 'Bogland', are the origin, the nurturing 'wet centre', of a subsequent manner and procedure and, in particular, of the major sequence of 'bog poems'.

The gaze which most obviously looks backwards in *Door into the Dark* also seems too self-consciously knowing. 'The Forge', that sonnet which uses another rural craft, the blacksmith's, as a further analogy for poetry, seems, as a result, already a study in a worn-out poetical fashion, over-insistent and *voulu*. For all the precision of evocation in some of the poem's details – that 'unpredictable fantail of sparks', for instance –

the real occupation tends to disappear behind its meta-
phorical significance: the 'forge' of the title seems, even
initially, less an actual forge than 'the quick forge and
working-house of thought' – the imagination, that is –
in Shakespeare's *Henry V*. The over-insistence shows, I
think, in the hyperbolically strained religious meta-
phor which makes the anvil 'an altar / Where he
expends himself in shape and music'; in the rather
facile opposition between the 'immovable' value pre-
sumed to inhere in the blacksmith's trade, and the
vulgarly 'flashing' traffic of the industrialized world
beyond the door-jamb; and in that sudden view of the
man himself, 'leather-aproned, hairs in his nose', and
grunting, which seems mere caricature. The excite-
ment of self-discovery evident in the earlier exercises
in analogy has congealed here into something al-
together too self-aware: 'The Forge', unlike 'The Diviner',
has too much the look of a poem that is looked at.
Which is why the less artificial 'Thatcher', which keeps
its eye firmly on its object, is more successful in releas-
ing, uninsistently, another analogy – the thatcher's
'Midas touch' – which, in its celebration of economy,
scrupulousness, a disciplined parsimony, anticipates
the characteristic strengths of *Wintering Out* and
North: the later manner is being advocated in a poem
which belongs, generically, to the earlier.

If rhyming 'to see myself' is, in some sense, a pro-
gramme for *Door into the Dark*, it does not, however,
imply any confessional directness. The 'buried life of
the feelings', and particularly of sexual feeling, is
certainly present in the book, giving it its fecund,
slippery, slightly voyeuristic character, with instances
of, and images deriving from, seed, intercourse and
generation, pregnancy, and the relationship between
men and women in marriage. Such 'feelings', however,
are not confessionally declared, but diverted through

[56]

metaphor, symbol, allegory, anecdote and dramatic monologue.

In the very different monologues, 'The Wife's Tale' and 'Undine', notions of the mutuality and inter-dependence of men and women are developed. In the realistic monologue of 'The Wife's Tale' – and perhaps the same could be said of 'Mother' – the touch is not always very certain. When Heaney speaks as a woman in these poems of *Door into the Dark*, it still seems very much his own voice doing the talking, and I am re-minded of Randall Jarrell's comment on Robert Lowell's 'The Mills of the Kavanaughs' – 'You feel, "Yes, Robert Lowell would act like this if he were a girl"; but whoever saw a girl like Robert Lowell?' The wife in 'The Wife's Tale' would talk like this – 'But I ran my hand in the half-filled bags / Hooked to the slots. It was hard as shot, / Innumerable and cool' – if she were Seamus Heaney; and she would talk like this – 'And that was it. I'd come and he had shown me / So I belonged no further to the work' – if she were Seamus Heaney imitating Robert Frost. That sudden veering of this presumably Irish wife's voice into the North of Boston accents of one of Frost's women is perhaps the technical sign of the poem's failure of empathy: for all that the men are 'grateful' in the poem's Breughelian closing line, there seems something too authoritatively directing in the husband, and too humbly subservient in her, for the monologue to ring altogether true as her account of the relationship.

The monologue-allegory of 'Undine' is more pro-tected from such a lapse. The 'undine' of Heaney's title is a female water-spirit who, by marrying a mortal and bearing him a child, might receive a soul – might, in other words, become human. In Heaney's account of the poem in 'Feeling into Words', he makes it 'a myth about agriculture, about the way water is tamed and humanized when streams become irrigation canals, when water becomes involved with seed'; but the monologue of the undine is the voice of a woman responding sexually to a man, describing an encounter which reaches its climax and resolution in an evocation of sexual interdependence:

> I swallowed his trench
> Gratefully, dispersing myself for love
> Down in his roots, climbing his brassy grain –
> But once he knew my welcome, I alone
>
> Could give him subtle increase and reflection.
> He explored me so completely, each limb
> Lost its cold freedom. Human, warmed to him.

The poem has, like 'The Wife's Tale', its element of male presumption: that 'Gratefully' is placed so prominently as to make it seem altogether too deferential. Nevertheless, this monologue does also articulate the woman's own proper pride, making her gratitude commensurate with his dependence on her – for the 'increase' of, presumably, sexual tumescence, his own sense of himself, and the possibility of a child, with its more than merely narcissistic 'reflection' of him. As the monologue of a water-spirit, 'Undine' is, perhaps, the spring's answer to the 'big-eyed Narcissus' who stares into it in 'Personal Helicon'.

In the volume as a whole, however, these satisfactions of mutuality are complemented by the darker sexuality of 'A Lough Neagh Sequence'. Heaney reprints almost the whole of this in his *Selected Poems*, and I can see why he admires it without myself admiring it so much. It gives him his first opportunity for an organized form more ample than the individual lyric, an attempt renewed frequently, in different ways, in his later work; and it gives him a weird and compelling subject – the life cycle of the eels and the work cycle of

the fishermen on Lough Neagh in Northern Ireland –
which may also act, as it moves through proverb,
legend, realism and 'visionary' transmutation, as a
kind of objective correlative for the compulsions of
human sexuality.

The sequence certainly manages to conjure 'eelness',
as Heaney has said (in the uncollected 'Deep as
England') Hughes's 'The Thought-Fox' manages to con-
jure 'foxness', in the slithering 'insinuating pull' of its
language and forms. The mysterious inexorability of
the eel's life cycle also clearly has its intimate symbolic
connection with the major themes of the book: when
'Dark / delivers him hungering / down each undulation',
the eel is acting as the submerged representative of the
book's various kinds of darkness.

There are several signs in the sequence, however,
that a significance greater than it can relaxedly bear is
being attached to the activity of eel fishing. There is the
over-elaborate patterning with 'Celtic' motifs of circu-
larity (further emphasized in the poem's original
pamphlet publication, when it was actually illustrated
with such motifs). When this patterning embraces every-
thing from the way 'Up the Shore' begins and ends with
the same line, to the wakes of the boats in 'Lifting', which
are 'enwound as the catch / On the morning water', it
comes to seem only decoratively applied to its material,
rather than intimately congruent with it. There is the
attempt at a sinewy, rippling kind of free verse in
'Beyond Sargasso' and 'The Return' (the former
actually imitating the eel's undulations typographically
when it pulls apart from itself in the middle). Although
this form may look appropriate to its occasion, it
betrays its lack of rhythmical subtlety in its un-
certainty about line-endings: what should, presum-
ably, undulate and writhe, in fact comes across as
hiccupingly staccato. There is, finally, in the climactic

poem 'Vision', something strained and portentous, as
the passing of the eels across land is made slippery
with adolescent sexual disgust: the eels are 'like
hatched fears', and watching them is said to have

> Re-wound his world's live girdle.
> Phosphorescent, sinewed slime
> Continued at his feet. Time
> Confirmed the horrid cable.

This has an element of the histrionic; and its failure
shows up especially in the word 'horrid'. I presume this
is intended to bristle with something of its etymological
derivation from the Latin *horridus*, 'revolting and
dreadful'; and some of Heaney's work does make a real
poetry out of the sudden restoration of evaporated
meanings (his use of the word 'nice' in 'The Last Mum-
mer', for instance). Here, however, the overworked
context militates against any such restoration; and
'horrid' seems only the word of childish irritability,
making the poem's conclusion lame and lopped, at once
enervated and melodramatic. Whatever dark stuff is
gestating in 'A Lough Neagh Sequence' is dragged
much more successfully into the light of articulation in
the bog poems, where – whatever else they are made to
represent – P. V. Glob's photographs provide another
'objective correlative' for hidden sexual feeling.

Gallarus Oratory, on the Dingle peninsula in Co. Kerry,
is a tiny monastic chapel built in the early medieval
period. When Heaney enters it in 'In Gallarus Oratory',
he senses a 'core of old dark'; and in 'Whinlands', 'Shore-
line', 'Bann Clay' and 'Bogland', this 'old dark' of history
and prehistory begins to be read out of the Irish landscape,
in a way that points forward to some of the central poems
in the two subsequent volumes, *Wintering Out* and *North*.
   'Whinlands' and 'Shoreline' may owe something to

another element in Ted Hughes, as it is apparent in the poem 'Thistles' in his volume *Wodwo*, of 1967. Hughes imagines his thistles as a kind of vegetal persistence of the spirit of Viking invasion:

> Every one a revengeful burst
> Of resurrection, a grasped fistful
> Of splintered weapons and Icelandic frost thrust up
>
> From the underground stain of a decayed Viking.
> They are like pale hair and the gutturals of dialects.
> Every one manages a plume of blood.

Heaney's whins ('gorse', in England) are similarly – although, it must be said, much less impressively – the emblematic inheritors of values attached to the history of a specific landscape:

> Gilt, jaggy, springy, frilled,
> This stunted, dry richness
> Persists on hills, near stone ditches,
> Over flintbed and battlefield.

The 'whinlands' characteristic of Northern Ireland become there – as Hughes's thistles do – the name for the persistence of a particular kind of culture and character. In 'Shoreline', Heaney receives the first of those visitations from the Vikings which are to constitute part of the mythology of *North*: 'Listen. Is it the Danes, / A black hawk bent on the sail?' The Vikings are present not in the vegetation of Ireland, but in the tide 'rummaging' at its coastline: Heaney's ear has perhaps been schooled to hear them, however, by Hughes's 'Thistles', and also by another poem more directly about the Vikings in *Wodwo*, 'The Warriors of the North', where, among several images for their invasions, Hughes includes their desire for 'the elaborate, patient gold of the Gaels'.

In 'Bann Clay', the clay of the Bann valley is imagined as an ultimate or absolute in the landscape, towards which Heaney's own work aspires ('I labour / Towards it still. It holds and gluts'), and the poem is perhaps a less subtle version of 'Toome' in *Wintering Out*. 'Bogland' itself, however, which ends *Door into the Dark*, is not just the first attempt at a finer poem, but contains within itself the excitement of the capacity for further extension and development. Heaney told Robert Druce that 'Bogland' 'was the first poem of mine that I felt had the status of symbol in some way; it wasn't trapped in its own anecdote, or its own closing-off: it seemed to have some kind of wind blowing through it that could carry on'; and the wind did, of course, carry on, through the sequence of 'bog poems' initiated by 'The Tollund Man' and 'Nerthus' in *Wintering Out*, and brought to fulfilment in *North*.

'Bogland' could be regarded as a kind of answering, Irish poem to Theodore Roethke's American 'In Praise of Prairie', in which 'Horizons have no strangeness to the eye' and 'distance is familiar as a friend. / The feud we kept with space comes to an end'. That American pioneering spirit, which looks outwards and upwards, to fulfilment through movement, advance, exploration and openness, is countered by Heaney's negative definition of Irish geographical experience – 'We have no prairies / To slice a big sun at evening': 'we' look 'inwards and downwards', into the bottomless centre of our own history, recovering there the traces and treasures of previous cultures and peoples, as the bogland of Ireland literally contains historical and prehistorical evidence released by archaeology. In this sense, 'Bogland' is a celebration of what Heaney described to Monie Begley as 'a kind of Jungian ground': the bog acts as the memory of the landscape, just as the unconscious in Jung's psychology is the archetypal memory of the race.

The sense of excited possibility in 'Bogland', however, derives not only from Heaney's first use of the symbol which is to act so powerfully in subsequent poems, but also from the fact that this poem itself describes its own lack of closure or containment, in the act of describing its 'external' subject:

> The ground itself is kind, black butter
>
> Melting and opening underfoot,
> Missing its last definition
> By millions of years.

Describing the ground here, the poem is also describing itself: its own falling rhythms and constantly enjambed lines also 'melt and open', aware, perhaps, that the symbol of the bog itself will melt and open again. In embedding within itself a commentary on itself in this way, 'Bogland' initiates that process of almost constant self-commentary in Heaney's later work, most notably in *North*, and initiates, therefore, a much more sophisticated and subtle kind of Heaney poem. 'The Forge' is a poem which, in Heaney's own terms, does remain 'trapped in its own anecdote': the poem is too snug a fit for the metaphor; nothing remains inchoate or unreconciled; and the whole thing seems glazed with self-satisfaction, almost made for the practical criticism class. 'Bogland' is a much riskier kind of poem – tentative, exploratory, following its own instincts, testing its footsteps. In *Wintering Out*, Heaney's work clearly inherits this element of risk. Turning away from statement, assertion, the enforcing of a moral, his poems begin to turn inward on themselves, sometimes in an almost riddling self-delightedness; and they begin to take as theme their own material, language itself.

*

This movement is implied in *Door into the Dark* by two recurrent features of the book – the 'self-inwoven simile', or the reflexive image, and the characterization of Heaney-as-driver. Christopher Ricks, in an essay on Andrew Marvell (collected in *The Force of Poetry*, 1984), has noticed in Heaney, as in some other contemporary poets from Northern Ireland, a poetic figure shared with Marvell. The figure is one that William Empson once defined as the 'self-inwoven simile'. There are instances of it in *Death of a Naturalist* (such as 'The burn drowns steadily in its own downpour', in 'Waterfall'), but it is more common in *Door into the Dark*, and persists variously in the later work. Ricks does not catalogue all the occurrences in *Door into the Dark*; but the most significant seem to me to be the following: 'a wick that is / its own taper and light', of an eel, in 'The Return'; 'under the black weight of their own breathing' in 'In Gallarus Oratory'; 'The leggy birds stilted on their own legs, / Islands riding themselves out into the fog' and 'things founded clean on their own shapes' in 'The Peninsula'; 'The breakers pour / / Themselves into themselves' in 'Girls Bathing, Galway 1965'; the mosquitoes 'dying through / Their own live empyrean' in 'At Ardboe Point'.

These images connect, in *Door into the Dark*, I think, with the structural circularity or reflexivity in 'A Lough Neagh Sequence'; with that weird instance of metaphorical and syntactical reflexivity in 'Bogland', 'the eye . . . / / Is wooed into the cyclops' eye / Of a tarn'; and with those epigrammatically reflexive remarks in 'The Plantation', 'Though you walked a straight line / It might be a circle you travelled', 'And having found them once / You were sure to find them again', and its concluding stanza:

> You had to come back
> To learn how to lose yourself,
> To be pilot and stray – witch,
> Hansel and Gretel in one.

'The Plantation', indeed, even more thoroughly than 'Bogland', is a poem about itself, its Janus-face looking both at the wood and at the poem, all its statements held in a gently unresolved tension between the literal and the metaphorical. That stanza could be regarded almost as the 'philosophy' of this reflexivity in Heaney. Both pursuer and pursued, both in control and in surrender, the poet finds himself by losing himself in the language and in the form of his own poem.

In the characterization of Heaney-as-driver in *Door into the Dark*, the potential solipsism of the reflexive is given an accompanying poetic persona, as the perceiver is cut off from the object of perception by a car windscreen. In 'The Peninsula', the recommendation to 'drive / For a day all round the peninsula' is specifically dependent on your having 'nothing more to say', on being locked into your own silence; and the poem tellingly recreates the exhilaration of meditative solitary driving. 'Elegy for a Still-Born Child' discovers in a similar situation not exhilaration but the pain of loss, as the driver's consciousness is saturated in an awareness of the dead infant:

> I drive by remote control on this bare road
> Under a drizzling sky, a circling rook,
>
> Past mountain fields, full to the brim with cloud,
> White waves riding home on a wintry lough.

The poems 'Night Drive' and 'At Ardboe Point' complicate the characterization by being also love poems. In 'Night Drive', the solitude of the journey through

France is tense with the expectation of the company which will end it, and the strong sexual feeling is, with shy artfulness, diverted into evocations of the drive itself – the signposts which 'promised, promised'; the places 'granting . . . fulfilment'; the thought of Italy laying 'its loin to France on the darkened sphere'. 'At Ardboe Point' modifies the figure: not now a solitary driver, but a pair of lovers together in the car, although curiously isolated nevertheless, at the centre of 'A smoke of flies' – 'they open and close on us / As the air opens and closes'. Even 'Shoreline', for all its recovery of a history of invasion from the Irish coastline, and for all that it eventually swells to embrace the whole island of Ireland, opens with a car 'Turning a corner, taking a hill / In County Down'.

This characterization of the protagonist-as-driver which Heaney initiates in *Door into the Dark* features centrally in some of his most important later poems – including the dedicatory poem of *Wintering Out* ('This morning from a dewy motorway'), 'The Tollund Man', 'Westering', 'The Toome Road' and the final poem of *Station Island*, 'On the Road'. It marks a move towards a more realistic reconciliation between the rural and the industrial or mechanical than the facile and sentimental oppositions implied by 'The Forge' – a sentimentality perhaps likely to tempt most 'rural' poets, and which seems to me to debilitate the work of some otherwise good writers who share territory in common with Heaney (George Mackay Brown, for instance). The sense it conveys of a consciousness hermetically sealed off from its perceived environment and circumstances is also partly responsible for that poignant loneliness which is such a notable feature of some of Heaney's most interesting work. 'Something of his sad freedom / As he rode the tumbril / Should come to me, driving', he says in 'The Tollund Man'; and an element of this 'sad freedom' inheres in most of these driving poems, even in *Door into the Dark*.

In his *Crane Bag* interview with Seamus Deane, Heaney explains that the poem 'Docker', about a Northern Protestant, and a poem about Carrickfergus Castle (a former bastion of English power in Ireland) were among his first mature poetic efforts: 'my first attempts to speak, to make verse, faced the Northern sectarian problem. Then this went underground and I became very in-fluenced by Hughes and one part of my temperament took over: the private County Derry childhood part of myself rather than the slightly aggravated young Catholic male part.' It did not go completely under-ground, however, even in the first two books, since *Death of a Naturalist* contains 'Docker', with its prophetic second stanza ('That fist would drop a hammer on a Catholic – / Oh yes, that kind of thing could start again'); and, in *Door into the Dark*, 'A Lough Neagh Sequence' (with its dedication, 'for the fishermen') offers its tacit sympathy and support to the clandestine 'poaching' activities of the group of fishermen who frequently came into violent conflict, and into the law courts, with the British company which officially owned the rights to eel fishing on Lough Neagh. What lies behind the 'sectarian problem' is also articulated, in these books, in three poems devoted to specific moments of Irish history – the Famine of 1845 in 'For the Commander of the "Eliza"' and 'At a Potato Digging', and the 1798 rebellion of the United Irishmen in 'Requiem for the Croppies'.

'For the Commander of the "Eliza"' and 'Requiem for the Croppies' are both dramatic monologues, the for-mer spoken by the captain of a ship who sights a rowing boat of starving Irish off the coast of Co. Mayo, and the latter, from beyond the grave, by one of the rebels killed by the English at Vinegar Hill, in Co. Wexford, in 1798. It is significant that Heaney's early attempts at the dramatic monologue – a form he has used in variously inventive ways since – should include these empathetic recreations of characters involved in crucial Irish historical events. It is also significant that Heaney's first use in his work of an Irish word should be, in the 'Eliza' poem, 'bia', repeated three times in desperation: the word for 'food'. Both poems also adapt to their own purposes pre-existent documentary sources – Cecil Woodham-Smith's study of the Famine, *The Great Hunger* (1962) in 'Eliza', and an impassioned and harrowing account of 1798 published by a survivor, P. O'Kelly, in Dublin in 1842, his *General History of the Rebellion of 1798*, in 'Requiem for the Croppies'. A use of documentary source material is later essential to the procedures of *North*, where Heaney constructs his own myth to articulate the 'sectarian problem'.

A comparison between poem and source for 'Eliza' reveals Heaney powerfully transforming the bleak original into a testimony to the humane but hopeless decency of the commander who speaks. In his report of the sighting –

> O my sweet Christ,
> We saw piled in the bottom of their craft
> Six grown men with gaping mouths and eyes
> Bursting the sockets like spring onions in drills

– not only the desperation of the apostrophe to Christ and the grotesque, quasi-expressionist simile are Heaney's own, but so also is the numerical particularity of that 'six' (the original has merely 'a boatload'). When it is later reported that the men remain 'like six bad smells' to haunt the ship, the precision has done its work, conveying a kind of eerily discriminating accountancy not inappropriate to the English treatment of Ireland during the Famine.

'Requiem for the Croppies' was written in 1966, when Irish poets were commemorating the fiftieth anniversary of the Easter Rising of 1916. In what is to become a recognizably oblique way, Heaney celebrates not the Rising itself but what he considers its original seed in the rebellion of 1798. The boys of Wexford, or the 'croppy boys' (so named because they cropped their hair in the manner of the peasants of the French Revolution) were mercilessly killed by the English at Vinegar Hill. Heaney's poem makes its nationalist sympathies clear enough when its final line ('And in August the barley grew up out of the grave') suggests some kind of political resurgence (in the 'spirit of 1916'?) by stating its fact of seasonal renewal. The light, anapaestic, folksong rhythm of the line also suggests, perhaps, the legendary persistence, in the Irish folk and popular imagination, of the moment of possibility in 1798.

'At a Potato Digging' is the clearest manifestation in Heaney's early work of a truth the Northern Irish poet Paul Muldoon has expressed by saying that in Ireland 'everything is coming down with history'. What specifically comes down with history in this poem is the activity with which *Death of a Naturalist* itself opens, digging for potatoes. The poem is artfully constructed, in its four sections, to uncover how, to the eye of the historical imagination, the 1845 Famine, when the potato disastrously failed, remains as a 'running sore' infecting and blighting the activity of harvesting the potato crop. The present is made transparent to the past by the minatory and chilling puns which describe the diggers' fingers going 'dead in the cold', and their feeling 'Dead-beat' before lunch; and in the deft cinematic dissolve between the second and third sections, where the metaphorical description of potatoes in their pits as 'live skulls, blind-eyed' turns into the literal 'Live skulls, blind-eyed' of those starving to death in 1845.

The continuity between past and present is made clear too in the imagining of the relationship between Irish peasant, or agricultural labourer, and the earth as a propitiatory religion of 'the famine god'. Potato digging is a ritual of appeasement (with 'processional stooping', 'humbled knees' and the labourers making 'a seasonal altar of the sod') to the earth as 'the black / Mother', the beneficent provider of food. When the crop fails during the Famine, the black mother is 'the bitch earth'; and, although the mother is subsequently partially demythologized as 'the faithless ground', the workers still spill their sacrificial 'Libations of cold tea'. The poem's rituals make it clear how deeply the sufferings of Irish historical experience are inscribed in the landscape itself and in the human psyche; and that 'black mother' will reappear in *Wintering Out* and *North*, in a newly mythologized form, as the goddess Nerthus.

III

Cold Beads of History and Home:
Wintering Out (1972)

It is a phrase associated with cattle, and with hired boys also. In some ways, it links up with a very resonant line of English verse that every schoolboy knows: 'Now is the winter of our discontent'. It is meant to gesture towards the distresses that we are all undergoing in this country at the minute. It is meant to be, I suppose, comfortless enough, but with a notion of survival in it.

> Seamus Heaney, explaining his title
> (*Listener*, 7 December 1972)

When it appeared in 1972, *Wintering Out* received a number of rather indifferent reviews. Some lamented its apparent inability to move far beyond the subject matter of the first two books, while others regretted its lack of any obvious engagement with the political situation in the North of Ireland: 'the bog oak, turf-banks and cobbles prevail', said the anonymous reviewer in the *Times Literary Supplement*, 'and no one is plucking up the latter to throw them at anyone'. Heaney had been writing, and publishing, poems which more straight-forwardly confronted the Northern violence after 1969, and some of them eventually reappeared in *North*; but *Wintering Out*, like its title, 'gestures towards' the realities of the present historical moment rather than attempting to address them with any specificity or intimacy. In the kinds of gesture it makes, however, it does genuinely address, if not the conflict itself, then the context out of which that conflict sprang. It is certainly possible to see with hindsight that, in doing so, it displays that peculiar charge and vibrancy, that excited stirring of confidence, which are the essential signatures of a truly individual talent coming, for the first time, into possession of its own unique identity. Apart from a handful of poems which seem written in an earlier manner ('First Calf', 'May' and 'Fireside'), *Wintering Out* is a volume in which a poet of outstanding distinction seems, in taking command of his proper material, hardly able to keep up with himself: it is a volume in which the promise of future work is almost as satisfying as the recognition of present achievement.

The reasons for Heaney's chosen obliquity are implicit in two of the poems in the book which come closest to the contemporary violence – the dedicatory poem, 'This morning from a dewy motorway' (which reappears as section IV of 'Whatever You Say Say Nothing' in *North*), and 'A Northern Hoard'. The dedicatory poem situates Heaney once more behind a car windscreen, driving past the new internment camp, Long Kesh (now known as the Maze), outside Belfast, built to house those picked up after the introduction of internment without trial in August 1971. Heaney is now cut off from the landscape not only by the car window, but by the sense that what he is seeing for the first time has actually been already seen: 'There was that white mist you get on a low ground / and it was déjà-vu, some film made / of Stalag 17, a bad dream with no sound.' That 'déjà-vu' is the register of Heaney's anguished bafflement: the internment camp is as unlikely, in this familiar territory, as a Nazi concentration camp; it has defamiliarized the locale. Yet it is utterly familiar too, in all the received images of the Second World War it summons to mind. How is something so estrangingly familiar to be described with any of the newness necessary to poetry? One cannot simply describe again what has already been described once too often; and this poem, indeed, takes refuge in the public language of the stoically witty graffito, 'Is there a life before death?' In 'A Northern Hoard', Heaney actually asks himself the question about poetry more directly: 'What do I say if they wheel out their dead? / I'm cauterized, a black stump of home.' 'Cauterized': seared into insensibility, incapable of feeling or responding, having nothing to 'say'. *Wintering Out* attempts to find a voice for this abjection, and to find images of suffering, endurance and resistance which will not seem already seen.

It searches for this voice and these images within that 'home' itself. In the final poem of 'A Northern Hoard', 'Tinder', Heaney remembers trying to strike fire from flints when he was a child. Developing the memory into a symbolically resonant reaction to the present, he imagines these flints as 'Cold beads of history and home' which he 'fingered'. This memorial rosary may act as an image for the poems in *Wintering Out* too, which intimately finger and fondle memories, objects, names and words from Heaney's own first world, in order to evoke it now in its historical, political and linguistic complexity. In fingering such 'cold beads of history and home', Heaney writes, in *Wintering Out*, a poetry everywhere bruised by Northern politics, even though rarely confronting them directly. His obliquities are not evasive: they are, on the contrary, subtly responsive and alert to present conflict; but concerned to be poetry, and not some other thing. As a result, the poems themselves hover intricately between the literal and the symbolic, between realism and allegory, between politics and philology. Restlessly missing their last definition, they avoid the snares of ideological declaration and received opinion. Instead, they feel tentatively along the lines that bind an individual to his people and a people to their history.

The historical and political theme in *Wintering Out* is carried, in a number of poems in Part One, by particular imagined or recalled human figures: Edmund Spenser, the 'moustached dead' and the 'geniuses' of wood and glen in 'Bog Oak'; the 'servant boy' of the poem containing the phrase which gives the book its title; 'the last mummer'; Shakespeare's MacMorris and Joyce's Leopold Bloom in 'Traditions'; the 'girl from Derrygarve' in 'A New Song'; Henry Joy McCracken, executed after the 1798 rebellion, who is alluded to in 'Linen Town'; 'the Tollund man'; and the labourer of 'Navvy'. They are complemented, in mood and meaning, by various figures in Part Two, with its more miscellaneous poems: the 'mother of the groom'; the mad girl of 'A Winter's Tale'; the resentful wife of 'Shore Woman'; the mermaid (or suicide?) of 'Maighdean Mara'; the mother who drowns her baby in 'Limbo'; the dumb victim of parental cruelty in 'Bye-Child'.

In both parts of the book, many of the evoked figures suffer some kind of human diminishment: isolation, repression, disenchantment, exploitation or betrayal. They act as exemplars of suffering and endurance, and they are, in a sense, fulfilled in the volume's two references to Christ: at the end of 'Limbo', where he is a figure of the most intense exclusion and ineffectualness ('Even Christ's palms, unhealed, / Smart and cannot fish there'), and in the quasi-surrealist final line of 'Westering' – and therefore of the whole book – where, in an image of lonely unconnectedness, Heaney imagines 'Christ weighing by his hands' in the moon's gravity.

In 'Navvy', Heaney addresses the labourer who 'has not relented / under weather or insults' as 'my brother and keeper'; but Heaney himself could be thought to act as the brother and keeper of his characters in 'Bog Oak', 'Servant Boy' and 'The Last Mummer', where he gives a place in poetry to those who have usually been excluded from it. In 'Bog Oak', he meditates on that familiar Irish building material, oakwood retrieved from bogland, and derives from it a colonial history in which the great poet of Elizabethan England, Edmund Spenser, is heavily implicated. As well as being the author of *The Faerie Queene*, that epic celebration of Elizabethan monarchy, Spenser was also one of the 'undertakers' in Ireland for the settlement of Munster; and in this capacity, in about 1598, he wrote his prose account of the Irish 'problem', *A View of the Present State of Ireland*, from which 'Bog Oak' quotes a phrase on the starving Irish peasantry. Heaney's sympathy in the poem is clearly not with Spenser, but with those historically dispossessed and maltreated, and with their successors, 'the moustached / dead, the creel-fillers'. As a poet writing in the English language, Heaney is inevitably part of the poetic tradition which also contains *The Faerie Queene*; but 'Bog Oak' suggests how tangentially and suspiciously related to it he is when it reminds us that such literary perfections as that great Renaissance poem – written by Spenser 'dreaming sunlight' in Kilcolman Castle, his planter's estate in Co. Cork – were the flower of a culture whose roots lay in the brutal political realities described in the *State of Ireland.*

Nevertheless, 'Bog Oak' is more saddened than resentful: it has, like those creel-fillers, its own 'hopeless wisdom'. 'Servant Boy', however, gives resentment its voice: the boy – servant, presumably, to one of the Big Houses of the Protestant Ascendancy – keeps a wily 'patience' and 'counsel', but ends 'resentful / and impenitent', a servant entirely without servility, carrying those eggs which may be 'warm' with the possibility of a different kind of future. In 'The Last Mummer', resentment breaks out into retaliation: the mummer, as the 'last' representative of the dying forms of rural life, 'trammelled / in the taboos of the country', casts his stone in anger at one of the homes in which the culture of television has disinherited him.

These poems also, however, imply Heaney's own kinship, as a poet, with his representative figures. Being watchful and alert is a wise recommendation for a poet as well as for a last mummer if both are 'picking a nice way through / the long toils of blood / / and feuding'; and, in the central stanza of 'Servant Boy', poet and character almost merge at the centre of their respective trails – the boy's wintering journey, the poet's written script:

> . . . how
> you draw me into
> your trail. Your trail
>
> broken from haggard to stable . . .

Heaney has been fond of quoting Robert Frost's dictum that, 'like a piece of ice on a hot stove, the poem must ride on its own melting'; and one of the characteristic effects of the new quatrain form he is inventing in these poems is of the melting, merging, dissolving of line into line and image into image, the poem perilously and precariously maintaining a grip on its own speedy unravelling. In that almost, as it were, palindromic line in 'Servant Boy' ('your trail. Your trail'), this process perhaps reaches a vanishing point; but it does suggest how useful the form could be to Heaney as an almost typographical enactment of sympathetic involvement with his subject, a testing, probing, tentative scrutiny of his material. In these poems of *Wintering Out*, this effect of the quatrain is reinforced by the beginnings of that use of the personal pronoun which is a vital element in the character of the poems of Part I of *North*: the poet's 'I' is detached from ordinary social circumstance, withdrawn to solipsistic meditation, ruminatively entranced, the hero of its own imaginative constructions and elaborations. We might think of it, in fact, as 'mythologized'.

Such a use of the personal pronoun, and the slim quatrain form, contribute to the effect of 'The Tollund Man', which could be regarded as the culmination of these poems of representative figures in *Wintering Out* – making it clear, indeed, that they constitute a kind of hagiography – as well as the initiation of the sequence of bog poems which follows in *North*. That the Tollund man has a similar sort of resonance for Heaney as the other figures of the book is made plain in the interview with James Randall where he says that when he first saw the man's photograph in P. V. Glob's book, *The Bog People*, he 'seemed like an ancestor almost, one of my old uncles, one of those moustached archaic faces you used to meet all over the Irish countryside'. One of the 'moustached dead' too, then; and we might remember that Heaney had already in fact written a poem about one of these old uncles, 'Ancestral Photograph' in *Death of a Naturalist*. I think there is some special pleading in Heaney's account, in this interview, of the Tollund man's photograph: the man is not very obviously 'moustached', and he is younger and more elegant, in fact, than such moustached, archaic Irishmen seem to me. This perhaps only makes it clearer, however, how much Heaney wants 'The Tollund Man' to be, in some sense, also a poem about an ancestral photograph: he is beginning, here, to discover, or to invent, that suggestive analogy between Glob's bog-bodies and the victims of Irish political violence which culminates in the extended mythologizing of the 'bog poems' of *North*.

The analogy is not dependent, of course, only on physical appearance; and Heaney emphasizes the deeper imaginative connection he is making when he publishes, alongside 'The Tollund Man', the very short poem 'Nerthus' (as he does again in his *Selected Poems*). Nerthus is the fertility goddess to whom, Glob argues, some of the Iron Age people dug out of the peat bogs of Jutland were ritual sacrifices: their murder in winter, and the disposal of their bodies in bogs sacred to the goddess, would ensure the fertility of the crops the following spring. This is why the Tollund man is, in Heaney's account, a 'Bridegroom to the goddess', and why the processes of his burial and preservation are described in sexual terms. It is also why 'Nerthus' describes the grains of the ash fork 'gathering to the gouged split': in the photograph of the representation of the goddess Heaney has in mind here, this 'split' is a heavy incision, symbolic of the female sexual organ, cut at the fork of a long, slim wooden branch. The poem, however, implicitly translates the goddess out of Iron Age Jutland into modern Northern Ireland when the landscape she stands in is defined in the terms of Northern dialect – 'kesh', a causeway, and 'loaning', an uncultivated space between fields: the former, in particular, taking an edge from its use in the proper name 'Long Kesh', the internment camp Heaney drives past in the dedicatory poem of the book.

This compacting in Heaney's imagination of Jutland and Ireland was impelled, he tells us in 'Feeling into Words', by his sensing a kinship between these ancient sacrificial killings and 'the tradition of Irish political martyrdom for that cause whose icon is Kathleen ni Houlihan' – for, that is, the cause of Irish Republicanism. The implications of this recognition are fully pursued in *North*; but in 'The Tollund Man' it gives Heaney his first opportunity to bring into relation the

Iron Age victim and the victims of recent Irish sectarian atrocity. In this imagined continuity of sacrificial ritual, the Tollund man is worked to 'a saint's kept body' by the preservative powers of the peat. He is therefore like the miraculously incorrupt bodies of Catholic hagiology, and may be prayed to as a saint is prayed to in Catholic worship: he may make these recent dead 'germinate' again, as his original killers hoped he would make their next season's crops germinate.

This notion has almost the startling force of a metaphysical conceit when it irrupts into the second section of the poem – the poetic equivalent, perhaps, of the religious danger of 'blasphemy' which Heaney invokes himself. However, although the analogy it suggests clearly provides the poem with its structure and its rationale, the connection which actually supplies its emotional sustenance is not that between Ireland and Jutland, but that between the Tollund man and Heaney himself. Heaney's 'mythologized' 'I' appears twice in the poem's opening section, in the repeated solemnity of a promise of pilgrimage; and the section lovingly and scrupulously disinters the man's body, carrying him from the photograph into language. The opening line of the second section – 'I could risk blasphemy' – is an admission of the man's power over him: he can compel a 'religious' reaction outside the norms of any conventional piety. And the third section, which prophesies Heaney's feelings when he gets to Jutland, establishes him and the Tollund man in exactly that kind of sympathetic relationship apparent also in 'Servant Boy'. Indeed, the 'trail' of that poem could be thought to survive here as Heaney's drive through the alien countryside, during which he shares the man's 'sad freedom' on the tumbril ride to his execution.

It is this empathetic involvement which produces the curiously dreamlike quality of the poem's well-known paradoxical concluding lines – both estranged and familiar, like the 'déjà-vu' of the book's dedicatory poem:

> Out there in Jutland
> In the old man-killing parishes
> I will feel lost,
> Unhappy and at home.

What the analogy has ultimately provided for Heaney in 'The Tollund Man' is this use of the word 'home', which goes beyond irony and sadness into tragedy, as comfortless and desolating as one could well imagine (although it perhaps has its parallel in Derek Mahon's 'Afterlives', which despairingly rhymes 'home' with 'bomb'). The lines are the more blankly disconsolate for the blunt archaic abruptness of that 'man-killing', which strikes virtually with the peculiarity of neologism when one remembers that it is ousting the more conventional (and almost metrically identical) 'murderous'.

In placing its emotional weight where it does, on the relationship between poet and evoked human figure, 'The Tollund Man' both inherits from some apparently less complex poems in *Wintering Out*, and also dissolves its more ambitious mythical elements into something sharply immediate: the pain of personal incomprehension, isolation and pity.

Part of the dislocating effect of the final section of 'The Tollund Man' derives from Heaney's imagining himself uttering an alienating litany while driving through Jutland:

> Saying the names

Tollund, Grauballe, Nebelgard,
Watching the pointing hands
Of country people,
Not knowing their tongue.

'Tongue' is a word that reverberates through *Wintering Out*, and the saying of other names – Anahorish, Toome, Broagh, for instance – is a common activity in the book. Not knowing the 'tongue' of the country you travel in is the deepest kind of estrangement; and Heaney's preoccupation with the tongue, in this book which subtly registers the contours of a divided culture, derives from the fact that the tongue he speaks, and uses as a poet – English – is not native or original to the land he comes from – Ireland – or straightforwardly identifiable with the feelings or aspirations of the tribe to which he belongs. English is the imposition of the colonial oppressor, dispossessing the native Irish of their own first 'tongue'. The historical and political themes of *Wintering Out*, therefore, are necessarily implicit in the actual tongue spoken in Northern Ireland; and the book includes many poems about language itself.

'Traditions' acts, perhaps even in a slightly self-conscious and programmatic way, as the major enunciation of this linguistic theme. A densely packed poem, it is centrally preoccupied with Shakespeare. Its first section imagines Elizabethan English as that 'alliterative tradition' ('alliterative', because the earliest metres of English poetry, in Anglo-Saxon and Middle English, were alliterative in form) which, following the Elizabethan Plantation of Ireland, has 'bulled' – raped, masculinely forced its will upon – the 'guttural muse' of the native Irish language, that virtually disappeared tongue commemorated in the beautiful, poignant, glancingly allegorical elegy, 'The Backward Look', which immediately precedes 'Traditions'. In the lines in which the initial act of rape is followed by acceptance of 'custom, that "most / sovereign mistress"' who 'beds us down into / the British isles', Heaney is drawing on *Othello* 1.iii, where the Duke calls opinion 'a sovereign mistress of effects', and Othello begins his reply, 'The tyrant custom . . . / Hath made the flinty and steel couch of war / My thrice driven bed of down'. The first section of 'Traditions' is therefore adapting Shakespeare to create a linguistic/sexual metaphor for Ireland's traumatic colonial history, a history whose crucial moment occurred during Shakespeare's lifetime.

The second section then ironically notes some of the contemporary results of this 'bulling' – the persistence, in the English spoken in Northern Ireland, of some 'correct Shakespearean' forms, and the currency of terms introduced by the Scots and English planters ('bawn', an English colonist's fortified farmhouse; and 'mossland', the Scots word for 'bogland': the forms are combined in the name of Heaney's first home, 'Mossbawn', which is why they are chosen as representative here). The third part of the poem focuses its theme through two further emblematic figures – not now invented, or imaginatively elaborated from their sources, but quoted from literature: Shakespeare's MacMorris from *Henry V* and Joyce's Bloom from *Ulysses*. 'What ish my nation?' is MacMorris's brogue interruption, in the third act of *Henry V*, when he presumes that Fluellen, the Welshman, is about to criticize the Irish. (In *The Irish Novelists 1800–1850*, Tom Flanagan, to whom 'Traditions' is dedicated, calls MacMorris 'the first stage-Irishman'.) The Irish as 'anatomies of death' is a further reference to Spenser's *State of Ireland*, to the same passage, in fact, quoted in 'Bog Oak'.

These Elizabethan English versions, or 'traditions', of Irishry – the comic buffoon; the deliberately starved victim – are finally countered in the poem by Leopold Bloom, the hero of Ireland's great epic (written, of course, in English), James Joyce's *Ulysses*. In the 'Cyclops' episode of that book, the Jewish Bloom defends himself against an anti-semitic Irish nationalist by insisting that Ireland is his nation because he was born there. The simple assertive dignity of his declaration – emphasized by Heaney's giving it two verbs of articulation, 'replied' and 'said' – is a criticism of the national stereotypes exhibited in the poem, and an insistence on the achievement of the English language as it is spoken, and written, in Ireland. Bloom, written out of the juncture between modern Irish urban experience and the English language, reveals James Joyce inheriting the language of Shakespeare, the 'alliterative tradition', but bending it to a 'guttural' Irish idiom, to produce – out of a sense of the futility of the received wisdoms and clichés of nationality – his great modern novel. It is not surprising, given the use made of Bloom here, to find Heaney referring to Joyce as 'the great and true liberator' ('A tale of two islands'), and observing elsewhere that 'his achievement reminds me that English is by now not so much an imperial humiliation as a native weapon' ('The Interesting Case of John Alphonsus Mulrennan'). Heaney's poetry eventually engages more strenuously with Joyce in the final section of the 'Station Island' sequence.

However, to have to consider the language you speak as either 'humiliation' or 'weapon' is to be rendered peculiarly alert to it as the medium of a history and a politics; and the word 'ear' is also prominent in *Wintering Out*, as Heaney describes himself listening in to the language of his own first world. He lies 'with my ear / in this loop of silence' in 'Land'; he remembers himself as 'small mouth and ear / in a woody cleft, / lobe and larynx / of the mossy places' in 'Oracle'; and, in 'Gifts of Rain', he takes 'soundings' into the flooded landscape.

That poem is characteristic of the poise between realism and allegory in *Wintering Out*. It begins as an evocation of the flooding of the Moyola, the local river of Heaney's first home, and discovers, in the wading man's reaction to the flood, a compelling image of interdependence between man and land, an image of circularity and reflexivity: the man 'hooped to where he planted', the sky and ground 'running naturally among his arms / that grope the cropping land'. The knowledgeable intimacy of this mutuality is then imagined as 'a world-schooled ear' which can 'monitor' the language of the flood; and the poem pushes out of realistic evocation into allegory, as Heaney's mythologized 'I' pushes out of the poem's previous third persons:

> I cock my ear
> at an absence –
> in the shared calling of blood
>
> arrives my need
> for antediluvian lore.
> Soft voices of the dead
> are whispering by the shore
>
> that I would question
> (and for my children's sake)
> about crops rotted, river mud
> glazing the baked clay floor.

The 'absence' which Heaney's ear picks up there is that of the older native 'lore' of pre-colonial Gaelic civilization ('antediluvian', I presume, because prior to the flood of colonization): it is the lore of native history and tradition which those 'soft voices of the dead' might speak – 'soft', no doubt, because they are speaking 'guttural' Irish, as well as because they are ghosts. The parenthesis represents the poem's moral urgency: listening in to this lore is necessary to any more equitable future. When, therefore, the native Moyola river 'spells itself' in the flood of the final section, 'bedding the locale / in the utterance', its 'tawny guttural water' represents some new political possibility for Ireland: one that, in some harmonizing and reconciling way, will 'pleasure' the poem's 'I', making him a 'Dives', the paradigmatic biblical rich man, by establishing, on this divided soil, 'common ground'.

I have been spelling out this poem's allegory here, not allowing it to 'spell itself', and this is to damage it, since its method is a rich suggestiveness and implication, a language stirring vibrantly with possible meanings rather than settling into declaration. When, in 'A New Song' – where the Moyola again appears 'pleasuring' – Heaney does attempt a greater declarativeness, the result is more problematical. A meditation on the name 'Derrygarve' issues in stanzas which are explicit, but equivocal:

> But now our river tongues must rise
> From licking deep in native haunts
> To flood, with vowelling embrace,
> Demesnes staked out in consonants.
>
> And Castledawson we'll enlist
> And Upperlands, each planted bawn –
> Like bleaching-greens resumed by grass –
> A vocable, as rath and bullaun.

These are difficult lines, and they are glossed only partially by the essay '1972' in *Preoccupations*, where, discussing his beginnings as a poet, Heaney writes, 'I think of the personal and Irish pieties as vowels, and the literary awarenesses nourished by English as consonants. My hope is that the poems will be vocables adequate to my whole experience'. Unlike the flood over 'common ground' at the end of 'Gifts of Rain', however, the flooding of a staked demesne seems much more an act of aggression, curiously remote, in fact, from a 'vowelling embrace'. The politically loaded words 'rise' (as in 'Easter Rising'?) and 'planted' (acquired by an act of dispossession during the Plantation), and the military 'enlist', restrain the lines from any easily unitary vision. And, as several commentators have noted, the word 'must' is ambiguous: does it suggest an inexorable process, or is it an encouragement to action?

What is clear is the prophecy that the colonized territory of the Plantation will be resumed, in some way, by entering into a new relationship with the native culture, as the old bleaching-greens of the Protestant Ulster linen trade have been 'resumed by grass', have gone 'native' again. The 'new song' of the poem's title, as opposed to the 'old song' which Robert Emmet, in 1803, called the story of England's relations with Ireland, will be sung in 'vocables'; but the word as it is used in the poem is less conciliatory than in '1972': the examples given of the new 'vocable' are in fact the very old Gaelic words, 'rath' (a hill-fort) and 'bullaun' (a hollowed stone mortar, found on archaeological sites).

Reticent, or uncertain, about how this new song might ever come to be sung, this poem has its origins in the optimistic civil rights period in Northern Ireland: despite its ambiguities, its tone is light, even joyful, and it derives its politics from an encounter which is, initially, playful or amatory, and as animated as a meeting in folksong ('I met a girl from Derrygarve'). Its image of native 'river tongues' is at one with the way the poem makes the Moyola itself a kind of mouth, its 'stepping stones like black molars', just as 'Gifts of Rain' gave the Moyola a voice. Heaney is here perhaps partly playing with the ordinary metaphor, 'the mouth of the river', and drawing out some implications of Wordsworth's use of the word 'voice' in relation to water – 'the voice / Of mountain torrents', for instance, in Book V of *The Prelude*. In their conjuring of an articulate landscape, and in the almost erotically satisfying 'pleasuring' which this offers, these poems are clearly related to those shorter pieces which are among the most original poems Heaney has written, the 'place-name poems', 'Anahorish', 'Toome' and 'Broagh'.

In his 1977 interview with Seamus Deane, Heaney said of these poems:

> I had a great sense of release as they were being written, a joy and devil-may-careness, and that convinced me that one could be faithful to the nature of the English language – for in some senses these poems are erotic mouth-music by and out of the anglo-saxon tongue – and, at the same time, be faithful to one's own non-English origin, for me that is County Derry.

They are intended, then, as sudden, swooping retrievals of reconciliatory 'vocables' from within the etymology of the warmly cherished place-names of Heaney's first home, and they may have been sanctioned by the Gaelic tradition of *dinnseanchas* which Heaney defines in 'The Sense of Place' as 'poems and tales which relate the original meanings of place-names and constitute a form of mythological etymology'.

The 'devil-may-careness' of their composition is reflected in the casual assurance and insouciance of their effect, and in what might even be thought the audacity of their titles. The names of these small townlands of Co. Derry are made to register, in English poetry, with something of that defiant self-assertiveness shared by the otherwise scarcely known place-names which entitle Eliot's individual *Quartets* or Edward Thomas's 'Adlestrop': they insist that the importance of a place depends not on the world's having heard of it, but on its significance for the poet who writes it. This presumptuousness is the origin of the astoundingly inventive and fecund compression of these poems, as the place-name articulated by the tongue is made to yield, speedily, a local history. They are poems which rapidly seize a world from a word.

In 'Anahorish', the word is almost wooed by the poet lovingly celebrating its 'vocable' – 'soft gradient / of consonant, vowel-meadow': the shape of the landscape, which reconciles hill and meadow, is reconstituted in the word, which reconciles, with the 'consonant' of its English, the 'vowel' of its original Irish – 'anach fhior uisce', the 'place of clear water'. The world conjured from the word is one of an almost Arcadian freshness, the 'first hill in the world': 'first' because it is the hill of Heaney's first world, and because it is the site of a human continuity which allows him to imagine the farm workers of his childhood as primitive 'mound-dwellers', conveying a sense of what 'The Seed Cutters' in *North* will call 'our anonymities'.

'Toome', similarly but less innocently, recovers from the 'soft blastings' of its pronunciation 'a hundred centuries' of human habitation. Toome is situated in the Bann valley, the site of major archaeological finds, and one of the oldest inhabited areas in Ireland: hence the discovery of those 'torcs and fish-bones' in the souterrain (an ancient underground chamber, of a kind found frequently in Ireland) under the 'slab of the tongue'. But Toome was also one of the sites of the 1798 rebellion, and hence the military remains – 'flints, musket-balls' – of those eighteenth-century battles. Out of all this history and prehistory, Heaney imagines himself 'prospecting what new' (an odd usage, which would more normally read 'what's new') – attempting to search out, perhaps, that alternative cultural and political possibility intimated in 'Gifts of Rain' and 'A New Song'. In fact, however, the prospector's search culminates not in the 'new', but in the very ancient indeed, as Heaney imagines himself pushing further down

> till I am sleeved in

> alluvial mud that shelves
> suddenly under
> bogwater and tributaries,
> and elvers tail my hair.

That extraordinary, quasi-surrealist Medusa image probably owes something to the Medusa heads of Celtic Britain and Ireland, illustrations of which Heaney would have seen in Anne Ross's *Pagan Celtic Britain* (1967), a book he cites during his discussion of 'The Tollund Man' in 'Feeling into Words'. The image therefore suggests, as Blake Morrison has observed, that Heaney has here 'located his primeval, preliterate self' (*Seamus Heaney*, 1982, p. 44). The poem certainly establishes a condition of primeval intimacy with this terrain, a sense that the existence of this 'I' is coterminous with its knowledge of this place. Nevertheless, the knowledge seems not enabling, or releasing, but dangerous. You lose your footing when the mud 'shelves / suddenly', particularly when the line break enacts the shock of it; and those elvers retain the queasy power of that 'horrid cable' of eels in 'A Lough Neagh Sequence', whose first section mentions Toomebridge, and whose final section perhaps prefigures this Medusa image, when the child is warned that the lice in his hair will 'gang up / Into a mealy rope / And drag him, small, dirty, doomed / Down to the water'. The Medusa, of course, turned anyone who looked at her to stone.

Heaney's intimacy with his place is more simply

pleasurable and conciliatory in 'Broagh', which draws from its place-name (the anglicization of the Irish 'bruach', a riverbank) the opportunity for the release, in an English poem, of the actual dialect and pronunciation of the speech of Co. Derry. The first three lines of the poem all end with dialect words: 'rigs', for 'furrows', a word brought to Northern Ireland by the Scots planters of the seventeenth century; 'docken', a Scots and archaic English plural; and 'pad', for 'path'. Later in the poem 'boortrees', a variant of 'bourtrees', is the old Scots plural for the elder (Heaney makes a whole poem out of the word in the fifth of his 'Glanmore Sonnets' in *Field Work*). This very short poem, then, celebrates, along with the Irish-derived name of its title, the 'planted' words of the local dialect English; and, imagining the riverbank itself as an imitation, in nature, of the form of the word, Heaney delights in the exclusivity of the pronunciation of 'Broagh'. Describing 'that last / *gh* the strangers found / difficult to manage' is a way of keeping the place private to this community, even while releasing it into the public articulation of a poem, since every reader not from Heaney's own place will also find that last '*gh*' difficult, if not impossible, to manage.

If 'Broagh' wilfully excludes some readers, however, it does so to create a paradigm of a certain kind of inclusiveness. Discussing the poem in *Among Schoolchildren*, Heaney says that the word 'Broagh' is 'a sound native to Ireland, common to Unionist and Nationalist, but unavailable to an English person'. This community of pronunciation is an implicit emblem for some new political community; and it is in this sense that 'Broagh' has a significance in Heaney's work altogether disproportionate to its length. Exhilaratedly riding on its own melting, it acts as a linguistic paradigm of a reconciliation beyond sectarian division. And, as

Heaney told Seamus Deane, it was the search to re-
capture the experience of writing these place-name
poems which led him to undertake his translation of
the medieval Irish poem, *Buile Suibhne*.

Nevertheless, *Wintering Out* knows that it is easier
to find emblems and paradigms than it is to create
political realities; and 'The Other Side' (its title a
version of the phrase used by both Catholics and
Protestants to refer to each other, 'the other sort'),
utters its 'no, not yet' and its 'no, not there'. In that
poem, the frail possibility of connection between Cath-
olic and Protestant neighbours, mined in any case by
silences and embarrassments, is intruded upon by the
mutual exclusiveness of their religious languages – the
mournful litany of the Catholic rosary, and the Prot-
estant's Old Testament arrogance. The Catholic's re-
sponse to the Protestant's remark, 'It's poor as Lazarus,
that ground', joins tongue and ear together, uniquely
in the book, with an almost surrealistic effect: 'my ear
swallowing / his fabulous, biblical dismissal, / that
tongue of chosen people'. An ear swallowing a tongue is
an image of appalling engorgement, making it un-
surprising that when Protestant turns away from
Catholic, he leaves 'a wake of pollen / drifting to our
bank, next season's tares'. Those 'tares' are also,
ironically, biblical, deriving from the parable of the
sower in Matthew XIII, where they are set deliberately
among wheat by an 'enemy'. These are the tares and
the enmities which Heaney's next book, *North*, almost
exhausted beyond conciliatory gestures, attempts to
render into words and images.

It has been generally thought that Part Two of *Winter-
ing Out* is a falling off after the vigour and originality
of Part One; and I would agree that it is the earlier
poems which most clearly define the move forward in

Heaney's career which the book represents. Neverthe-
less, *Wintering Out* seems to me a more genuinely
shaped and structured book – hinting at the bipartite
form subsequently adopted by *North* – than has
usually been granted, and I think that, in one signifi-
cant respect, Part Two is needed to complete the mean-
ing of Part One.

I noted earlier that both parts share exemplary or
emblematic figures of suffering or endurance, those of
Part Two having a significant role in establishing the
chilly, disconsolate mood of the book. These latter
figures move out of prehistory, history and literature
into the contemporary world, although they acquire
something of an almost mythical or legendary quality
too. This is created largely by the imagery of moonlight
and sea in which they are bathed, and which they
share with 'Roots', the opening section of 'A Northern
Hoard' in Part One. There, the woman is, like one of
Henry Moore's Underground sleepers, 'moonstruck / To
drifted barrow, sunk glacial rock', and the poem's
gruesome symbolic mandrake is 'soaked by moonlight
in tidal blood'. In Part Two, the unhappy wife of 'Shore
Woman' walks in the moonlight to become almost
disembodied in the final line, 'A membrane between
moonlight and my shadow'; the mermaid-suicide of
'Maighdean Mara' lies in water, 'her cold breasts /
Dandled by undertow'; the victimized boy in 'Bye-
Child' is a 'Little moon man', his dumbness a 'gaping
wordless proof / Of lunar distances / Travelled beyond
love'. In the final poem of the book, 'Westering',
Heaney then sets himself under 'Rand McNally's /
"Official Map of the Moon"' in California, remembering
Donegal and the moon's 'bony shine' throwing his
shadow on whitewash, and imagining Christ 'weighing
by his hands' in the moon's 'untroubled dust' – unlike
the Earth's dust, we may take it, on which all of these

[92]

emblematic figures are personally 'troubled', and on which Ireland is undergoing its political 'Troubles'.

These lunar associations, and the poem's roads 'Falling light as casts / Laid down / On shining waters', suggest that Heaney is making himself, in 'Westering', one of his own emblematic figures. His drive across Ireland to 'The empty amphitheatre / Of the west' isolates and estranges him on his own home territory as, on Good Friday, he passes a succession of Irish congregations inside their 'still churches', he and his family only a 'dwindling interruption'. This provides the book, perhaps, with its final image of being 'lost, / Unhappy and at home', an image created 'six thousand miles away' from home, while imagining the utter alienness of the moon. In its lostness and unhappiness, the poem is a fitting close to *Wintering Out*; but its image of Heaney himself as estranged outsider is also appropriate to the personal, domestic distress evident in Part Two of the book, which complements the larger political and historical distress of Part One. It is in this primary sense that Part Two seems to me integral to the overall design of *Wintering Out*: the book's lostness and unhappiness are located, in the end, 'at home' – at, in fact, Heaney's 'Summer Home'.

The poem painfully evokes an unhappy period in a marriage by articulating images and emblems of un-ease, guilt, temporary assuagement, sexual desire and fulfilment, and sheer persistence. The personal material is gracefully deflected into the symbolic (the sourness of the marriage as the air 'possessed' by the undis-coverable but insistent presence of a mat 'larval' with summer insects); the glancingly mythologized (Heaney as an unlikely Proserpine, 'Bushing the door, my arms full / of wild cherry and rhododendron'); and the erotically intent ('as you bend in the shower / water lives down the tilting stoups of your breasts'): all are directed towards composure, rather than confession. The poem's final section, originally published under the title 'Aubade', is a very muted song for the arrival of dawn, but still a song, in which the domestic rancour is given its full weight, but is opposed, however timidly, by a continuing 'love':

> My children weep out the hot foreign night.
> We walk the floor, my foul mouth takes it out
> On you and we lie stiff till dawn
> Attends the pillow, and the maize, and vine
>
> That holds its filling burden to the light.
> Yesterday rocks sang when we tapped
> Stalactites in the cave's old, dripping dark –
> Our love calls tiny as a tuning fork.

The difficulties are formally dramatized in those lines by the heavy enjambments and caesurae which restrain the forward thrust of syntax: the future that the lines cry out to be released into is disrupted and postponed. The nervous irresolution of the pararhymes complements the effect; and they reach their painful diminuendo in the sadly dissonant chime of 'fork' against 'dark'. The whole perfectly managed thing is fulfilled in the perfection of its final simile, which looks forward, perhaps, to that other metallic simile for love at the end of 'Sunlight' in *North* – 'like a tinsmith's scoop / sunk past its gleam / in the meal-bin'. The little human noise resonating in the old dark of personal unhappiness and of humbling nature, as it has earlier resonated in the old dark of Irish historical and political experience, is the true note of *Wintering Out*: comfortless enough, but with a notion of survival in it too.

IV

The Appetites of Gravity: *North* (1975)

In Ireland at the moment I would see the necessity, since
I'm involved in the tradition of the English lyric, to take
the English lyric and make it eat stuff that it has never
eaten before . . . like all the messy and, it would seem,
incomprehensible obsessions in the North, and make it
still an English lyric.

> Seamus Heaney to Harriet Cooke, 1973

The decision to confront the crisis of Northern Ireland in
a more stringent way must have come to seem almost
inevitable to Heaney after the publication of *Wintering
Out*. Some of the reviewers of that volume clearly had
such an expectation; some of the poems he had published,
but not collected, did handle the subject more directly;
and his role as a public spokesman and commentator
was increasingly demanding both a scrutiny of his own
responses and position and a consideration of the kinds
of language appropriate to the occasion. The move from
Belfast to Dublin in 1972, particularly in the light of the
media commentary it received, no doubt gave these
compunctions a sharper edge and urgency, while it also
brought a perspective of at least geographical distance.
Above all, however, his anxieties about confronting the
subject had been mitigated by his discovery of Glob's
The Bog People and, in 'The Tollund Man', of a way of
using that material as analogy, of making it render
what he calls in 'Feeling into Words', 'images and

symbols adequate to our predicament'. As he explained to Brian Donnelly in 1977:

> My emotions, my feelings, whatever those instinctive energies are that have to be engaged for a poem, those energies quickened more when contemplating a victim, strangely, from 2000 years ago than they did from contemplating a man at the end of the road being swept into a plastic bag – I mean the barman at the end of our road tried to carry out a bomb and it blew up. Now there is of course something terrible about that, but somehow language, words didn't live in the way I think they have to live in a poem when they were hovering over that kind of horror and pity. They just became inert. And it was in these victims made strangely beautiful by the process of lying in bogs that somehow I felt I could make offerings or images that were emblems.

'The Tollund Man' obviously contained within itself the enabling seeds of further development.

At the same time, Heaney was reading – as his critical prose of the period makes clear – some modern and contemporary long poems, or poetic sequences: David Jones's *The Sleeping Lord* (published in book form in 1974, but available much earlier) and his *Anathemata* of 1952, Geoffrey Hill's *Mercian Hymns* (1971) and – a sequence developed out of, and responding to, the Northern experience – John Montague's *The Rough Field* (1972). These are poems which, variously, set personal experience in a larger cultural and historical context and, perhaps as a result, display a studied and deliberate interest in archaeology and etymology. They are poems which might be thought to retain, vestigially, some of the ambitions of 'epic' poetry, or to attempt some kind of synthesizing historical myth, a form in which the confusions of the present may be articulated and understood with what will seem a more than merely individual authority. An extension and elaboration of

the relationship between Ireland and Jutland discovered
in 'The Tollund Man' provided Heaney with the basis for
such a myth of Northern Ireland.

The sequence of 'bog poems' subsequently written
out of this perception ('Come to the Bower', 'Bog
Queen', 'The Grauballe Man', 'Punishment', 'Strange
Fruit' and 'Kinship') does lie at the centre of *North* –
at the centre of its meaning, of its effect, and of its
achievement. But the book's myth is also developed
from a variety of other sources. Separate poems medi-
tate not only on bodies but also on objects retrieved
from the Northern ground (quernstones, a Viking long-
ship, Viking trial pieces, a white bone, a spade covered
with moss, a turf cart), and on words retrieved from the
language spoken on that ground ('moss', 'bawn',
'Dublin', 'bone-house' or '*ban-hus*', 'bog'). These poems
uncover, in their meditations, a history of Ireland's
conquest, first by the Vikings and later by the English.
The myth is also advanced by poems in which the
concept of territorial conquest is itself allegorized in
terms of the Greek myths of Hercules and Antaeus,
and of Diana and Actaeon, and in sexual terms. More-
over, in 'The Digging Skeleton', the myth finds room
for a translation from Baudelaire of a poem about
anatomical drawings which imagines human misery
persisting beyond the grave: in a pointed oxymoron,
Heaney translates Baudelaire's word for the dead,
'forçats' (hard-labourers), as 'Death's lifers', which is
chillingly appropriate to the bodies preserved for so
long in the Danish bogs.

The myth, however, occupies, in the overall struc-
ture of *North*, only the first (if certainly the much
richer) of its two parts, the second of which contains
poems directly responsive to the Northern present,
rather than to its past. Perhaps initially deriving its
bipartite structure from that already adumbrated in

[97]

Wintering Out, North employs it to much more radical effect. Talking to Seamus Deane in 1977, Heaney emphasized the dichotomy in his own response as a poet:

> The two halves of the book constitute two different types of utterance, each of which arose out of a necessity to shape and give palpable linguistic form to two kinds of urgency – one symbolic, one explicit.

Elsewhere, he has elaborated this to include an account of the symbolist Part I as a Yeatsian 'heaven' of discourse, and the more explicit Part II as a Kavanagh-like 'home' of the rational and quotidian. Clearly, the distinction has its correlative in Heaney's own expressed responses as a citizen – in '1972', for instance, 'At one minute you are drawn towards the old vortex of racial and religious instinct, at another time you seek the mean of humane love and reason'; but the bipartite form of *North* is impelled primarily by Heaney's preoccupation with 'types of utterance'; and, following the remark I have quoted from '1972', he immediately turns to his own responsibilities as a poet: 'Yet is your *raison d'être* not involved with marks on paper? As Patrick Kavanagh said, a man dabbles in verses and finds they are his life.' In throwing attention on the nature of the 'utterance' itself, the structure of *North* makes it a profoundly self-conscious book.

This self-consciousness is apparent also in the way it places art itself, and Heaney's own art as a poet in particular, at its centre. The dedicatory poems under the title 'Mossbawn' evoke domestic and communal images of Heaney's own first Northern home, of human love and agricultural continuity, which recall Dutch and Flemish paintings. 'Sunlight', which remembers his aunt baking, has, with its composed stillness and its almost-archaism (dusting the board 'with a goose's

wing'), something of the atmosphere of an interior by
Vermeer (Robert Lowell once referred to 'the grace of
accuracy / Vermeer gave to the sun's illumination', and
Heaney's poem conjures a similar grace from its sun-
light). 'The Seed Cutters', celebrating 'calendar cus-
toms', directly addresses a painter – 'Breughel, / You'll
know them if I can get them true'. These painterly
images of beneficent tranquillity, of home-keeping and
community, remain, as it were, outside the frame of
North, implicitly commenting on the images of bar-
barism within the frame, particularly, perhaps, those
derived from other, harsher art works: the Viking
longship incised by the child as a trial piece in 'Viking
Dublin'; the anatomical plates of 'The Digging
Skeleton'; the Greek bronze of the conquered Celtic
warrior dying on his shield, known as 'The Dying
Gaul', alluded to in 'The Grauballe Man'; Goya's
'Shootings of the Third of May' and his image of 'that
holmgang / Where two berserks club each other to
death / For honour's sake, greaved in a bog, and sink-
ing' in 'Summer 1969'; and, perhaps, the bog people
themselves, iconically static in the frames of Glob's
photographs.

These allusions to the plastic arts are accompanied,
in *North*, by an extraordinarily high density of allusions
to other writing – literary, historical and political.
Occasionally very obviously signalled by quotation
marks or italics, or by their use as epigraphs, but
usually embedded more invisibly in Heaney's own
texts, these allusions include, among many others,
references to: the Norse myth of *Njal's Saga*; the
Roman historian Tacitus's accounts of the Northern
tribes in his *Germania* and *Agricola*; *Hamlet*; Joyce's
Portrait of the Artist; Synge's *The Playboy of the West-
ern World*; Bede's *History of the English Church and
People*; Yeats's poems and *Autobiographies*; Walter

Ralegh's 'Ocean's Love to Cynthia' and John Aubrey's account of Ralegh; Edmund Spenser's dictation of Lord Grey's account of the Battle of Smerwick; the Anglo-Saxon *Battle of Maldon*; Conor Cruise O'Brien's *States of Ireland*; Horace's odes; R. H. Barrow's *The Romans*; Wordsworth's *The Prelude*; Patrick Kavanagh; Hopkins's *Journals*; Osip Mandelstam. Given the nature of its primary subject – Northern Ireland in crisis after 1969 – *North* is an astonishingly literary book which foregrounds the way it turns its material into text (literally so in 'Bog Queen', where 'My body was braille / for the creeping influences' and in 'Kinship' with its 'hieroglyphic' peat).

These allusions are integral and organic, not merely ornamental. They are made partly, no doubt, in the spirit of Walter Benjamin's famous remark that 'There is no document of civilization which is not at the same time a document of barbarism'; but they are also made since *North* is a book almost as much about poetry itself as it is about Northern Ireland. The Greek myth of Hercules and Antaeus which encloses Part I in two separate poems is obviously primarily an allegory of colonization: in 'Hercules and Antaeus', Hercules is the stronger aggressor breaking the native Antaeus, son of Earth, by removing him from his source of strength in the ground and leaving him in the land in the shape of that persistent Celtic theme, the 'sleeping giant' who will one day awake to lead his people into their true inheritance – a desperate cultural escapism described brutally as 'pap for the dispossessed', the mythology which keeps an oppressed people hopeful but puerile. Talking to John Haffenden, Heaney acknowledged 'Hercules and Antaeus' as an allegory of Ireland, but also spoke of its rather different genesis:

> To me Hercules represents another voice, another possibility; and actually behind that poem lay a conversation

with Iain Crichton Smith, a very fine poet but essentially different from the kind of poet I am. He's got a kind of Presbyterian *light* about him. The image that came into my mind after the conversation was of me being a dark soil and him being a kind of bright-pronged fork that was digging it up and going through it . . . Hercules represents the possibility of the play of intelligence, that kind of satisfaction you get from Borges, the play and pattern, which is so different from the pleasures of Neruda, who's more of an Antaeus figure. That kind of thinking led into the poetry of the second half of *North*, which was an attempt at some kind of declarative voice.

In this reading, then, the allegory of Hercules and Antaeus is as much an allegory of poetry as of politics, as much an allegory of the bipartite structure of *North* itself as of the relationship between England and Ireland. The two allegories are, we might say, coterminous.

Indeed the poetic and the political are frequently coterminous in the book. Heaney as poet is present in Part I not only in the centrality of his 'I' (all those personal pronouns and possessive adjectives which open poems or sections of poems: 'I shouldered . . .', 'I returned . . .', 'Come fly with me', 'My hands come . . .', 'I can feel . . .', 'I found . . .'), but also in the fact that the poetry discusses or exposes its own processes of composition. In the audacious conceit of 'North' itself, the Viking longship's 'swimming tongue' is one of the earliest, and strangest, of the exemplary voices which counsel Heaney in his own poetry:

> It said, 'Lie down
> in the word-hoard, burrow
> the coil and gleam
> of your furrowed brain.

Compose in darkness.
Expect aurora borealis
in the long foray
but no cascade of light.

Keep your eye clear
as the bleb of the icicle,
trust the feel of what nubbed treasure
your hands have known.'

Heaney's fiction of being advised, in this way, by a Viking voice establishes a frightening intimacy between the sources of his poetry and the brutal facts of Viking culture and power. The speaking longship also, however, anticipates Heaney's later self-communings in *North*. When, in recommending that cold Nordic clarity of perception, it discovers its metaphor for poetic fulfilment in the 'aurora borealis', the Northern Lights, rather than in the sudden irruption of a 'cascade of light', it is articulating exactly the contrast of expectations which Heaney, more *in propria persona*, articulates in the final poem in *North*, 'Exposure', in the metaphors of 'falling star' and 'meteorite'. The poems therefore seem almost companion pieces; and their connection is further signalled by the verbal link between 'the hatreds and behind backs / of the althing' in 'North' and 'the anvil brains of some who hate me' and 'what is said behind-backs' in 'Exposure'.

In 'Viking Dublin', the 'darkness' of composition is illuminated when, between sections III and IV, the Viking child's incised drawing of the longship – 'a buoyant/migrant line' – visibly insinuates itself into Heaney's own script, as the longship 'enters my longhand, / turns cursive'. The effect perhaps inherits from the 'trail' of 'Servant Boy' in *Wintering Out*; but the greater self-referentiality here is almost the equivalent of that in an Escher drawing. The invitation it extends to the reader actually to enter the processes of the poem's composition is sustained in 'Bone Dreams', where Heaney describes himself burrowing in an Anglo-Saxon word-hoard, to retrieve a sense of the ancient culture from the word 'ban-hus'. In the bog poems, this poetic self-consciousness takes the form of an anxiety about making poems out of human suffering: the Grauballe man is an exemplary instance of the closeness between 'beauty and atrocity'; in 'Punishment', Heaney is an 'artful voyeur'; and in 'Strange Fruit', the beheaded girl resists all his poetic attempts at 'beatification' (as he had beatified the Tollund man in *Wintering Out*).

In Part I, however, the subtext of a poetry talking to itself about itself is perhaps most obvious in the fourth section of 'Kinship', where Heaney speaks of the bog in terms which turn it into a kind of language. The section alludes, in its opening line, 'This centre holds', to Yeats's 'The Second Coming', with its prophetic announcement that 'The centre cannot hold'; and, in the evocation of the bog's formation by autumnal decay, as it dies into its own life, there seems also to be an echo of Eliot's description of autumn in 'The Fire Sermon' from *The Waste Land* ('the last fingers of leaf / Clutch and sink into the wet bank'). This bog is, therefore, already almost a poem too before Heaney makes an identification which suggests an analogy between the self-involved processes of the bog and the self-involved processes of poetic language, that compost of allusion and etymology which generates the composition of the new work:

> This is the vowel of earth
> dreaming its root
> in flowers and snow,

mutation of weathers
and seasons,
a windfall composing
the floor it rots into.

I grew out of all this
like a weeping willow
inclined to
the appetites of gravity.

'Grew out of' in the sense of 'was derived from', but also, perhaps, 'grew away from'; 'inclined to' as 'bent towards', but also 'predisposed to': the stanza's own ambiguities compose the floor it rots into. And the willow unites, in its apt simile, the opposed inclinations: it grows away from, but is also bent back towards, the ground which sustains it. It is Hercules and Antaeus intertwined, and it is 'weeping' as an entirely understandable reaction to the 'all this' symbolized by the bog in *North*.

In Part II, this subtext rises to the status of text, as Heaney debates more openly the relationship between poetry and public life (in the 'declarative' voice of 'Whatever You Say Say Nothing', in the fantasy of 'The Unacknowledged Legislator's Dream', and in the allegory of 'Freedman') and as, in 'Singing School', he describes, in realistic terms and under the aegis of autobiographical epigraphs from Wordsworth and Yeats, what were the immediate social circumstances which he, Seamus Heaney, 'grew out of'. The final poem of 'Singing School', 'Exposure', then acts as a kind of coda to subtext and text when it anxiously rehearses this poet's responsibilities in the light of 'all this' and, in a context of allusion, brings *North* to an end on a note of sadness, exile and loss.

Guilty, anxious and uncertain, 'Exposure' is an entirely appropriate conclusion to a volume in which the poet's own art of composition has itself been the focus of so much attention. The attention manifests a scrupulous unease about the ways in which poetry – 'marks on paper' – may properly engage the obdurate facts of political violence and death. This scepticism, suspicion and lack of presumption seem to me the mark of the book's true authority. By confessing its own artfulness, *North* discovers and sustains a humility and a gravity genuinely responsive to the urgency and intractability of its occasion.

In the middle of 'Viking Dublin : Trial Pieces', immediately after the longship has entered his longhand, Heaney makes a half-mocking, half-serious self-identification:

> I am Hamlet the Dane,
> skull-handler, parablist,
> smeller of rot
>
> in the state, infused
> with its poisons,
> pinioned by ghosts
> and affections,
>
> murders and pieties,
> coming to consciousness
> by jumping in graves,
> dithering, blathering.

The myth of Part I of *North* is made from such death-infected identifications: Heaney constructs his 'parables' for the Irish present by contemplating objects, skulls and bodies retrieved from the ground and the grave. When 'Belderg' discovers, in the excavated Norse settlement in Co. Mayo, an exact replication of the 'stone-wall patternings' of the contemporary landscape, it describes this as 'persistence, / A congruence of lives'; and the whole of Part I is devoted to establishing a sense of these persistences and congruities. But it does so with the ironic knowledge that such an activity may be only 'blathering', that such word-spinning may be only a helpless, Hamlet-like incapacity for action.

The predominant effect of these poems is of an intense, almost claustrophobic obsessiveness and intimacy. The separate poems, sometimes in lengthy sequences, revolve very similar matters among themselves and, indeed, frequently share similar or identical images. The 'black glacier' of a funeral in 'Funeral Rites' reappears as the 'black glacier' of a sash in 'Bog Queen'; the 'neighbourly murder' of 'Funeral Rites' – that savage oxymoron – has its correspondence in the description of the Vikings as 'neighbourly, scoretaking / killers' in 'Viking Dublin'; the Bog Queen is wrapped in a 'swaddle of hides', and the decapitated girl of 'Strange Fruit' has her hair 'unswaddled' by her discoverer; the Bog Queen has 'dreams of Baltic amber' and, in 'Kinship', the word 'bog' itself is defined as 'pupil of amber'; and so on, through a number of other links and variations. This dangerous procedure makes a certain monotony part of its effect: the poems seem inverted, almost incestuously self-generated; and this is further emphasized, perhaps, by their being hermetically sealed off within the enclosing frame of the two Antaeus poems. The sense is powerfully conveyed of a sequence of poems bearing an exceptionally close family resemblance (I know I am not alone in finding it difficult, in memory, to tell them all apart); and this seems peculiarly appropriate to a sequence which includes a poem called 'Kinship' and which discovers an interconnectedness, a family resemblance, between contemporary sectarian atrocity in the North of Ireland, the behaviour of Viking invaders, and the ritual murders of Iron Age Jutland.

The intimate relationship between these poems is made clearest, however, by their most common form, the thin quatrain, now sometimes grown almost skeletal. It is heavily stressed, characteristically with two stresses to a line (like the half-line of Anglo-Saxon alliterative metre); it often breaks its line to coincide with the grammatical phrase; and it makes much use of that punctuation mark of pause, definition and weighed apposition, the colon (every single poem in the sequence has its colon or, in one or two cases, that quicker equivalent of the colon, the dash). As a result, it is far less airy and buoyant than its equivalent in *Wintering Out*, and it has a certain archaic quality, 'fretted rather than fecund', as Heaney says of Hopkins's forms in 'The Fire i' the Flint' in *Preoccupations*.

This 'frettedness' is increased by the characteristically resistant vocabulary of the poems: they refer to, quote, and imitate Anglo-Saxon 'kennings' (periphrastic noun phrases) in such usages as 'word-hoard', 'love-den', 'blood-holt', 'brain-firkin', 'oak-bone', 'mushroom-flesh', 'flint-find'; they use Northern dialect ('pash' for 'head', for instance) and words from the Gaelic ('crannog', 'pampooties', 'glib'); and they employ the precisions of technical vocabularies ('zoomorphic', 'obelisk', 'felloes'). The poems are not aggressive towards the reader, exactly, but neither are they accommodating: hard-edged, all elbows with their constantly jolting line breaks and dictionary diction, they do clearly disrupt the English lyric voice in a way appropriate to the violence of their material, and in a way which may also carry a weight of political resistance. As Heaney explained to Frank Kinahan, 'I thought that that music, the melodious grace of the English iambic line, was some kind of affront, that it needed to be wrecked.' This wrecking, or disruption, was probably sanctioned by Heaney's admiration for Robert Lowell's work of the late 1960s and early 1970s which practised violences upon the English sonnet; and there is, indeed, one moment in *North* when Heaney emulates, rather un-convincingly, a certain braggadocio element in some of those Lowell poems – when he says of Goya in 'Summer 1969' that 'He painted with his fists and elbows, flourished / The stained cape of his heart as history charged'.

Heaney was also, however, fascinated by the look of his quatrain forms on the page, by their typographical appearance. He told James Randall that 'those thin small quatrain poems, they're kind of drills or augers for turning in and they are long and narrow and deep'. The fallacy of imitative form in a particularly virulent condition, it may be thought; but, in a book so interested in the plastic arts, it is unsurprising that Heaney should have been encouraged by the fact that his forms themselves have the shape of archaeological im-plements, that they look like a means of returning to the light of human scrutiny what has lain so long underground.

In addition to establishing a link between the culture of the Vikings and Heaney's own writing in 'North' and 'Viking Dublin', as I have suggested, the Viking poems which open Part I of *North* also draw together, in a pattern of analogy, the violence of the Vikings and the violence of contemporary Northern Ireland. In 'Belderg', the images of persistence in the ancient and modern landscapes are matched by possible elements of con-tinuity in the name 'Mossbawn', when Heaney's com-panion in the poem suggests a Norse derivation for the word. The suggestion leads Heaney to a moment of vertiginous vision in which, in his 'mind's eye', he sees 'A world-tree of balanced stones, / Querns piled like vertebrae, / The marrow crushed to grounds.' That 'world-tree' is the Yggdrasil of Norse mythology, the ash tree which sustained the Viking world in being. In

Heaney's vision, its sustaining power is terror and savagery; and the vision is a hideous reversal of the images of sunlight and community which go under the name 'Mossbawn' in the book's dedicatory poems.

'Funeral Rites' similarly yokes together the funerals of Heaney's own childhood, the present funerals of victims in the North, and the burial of Gunnar, one of the heroes of the Norse *Njal's Saga*. It is the phrase 'neighbourly murder' which establishes the connection between present and past: those who are 'neighbours' in Northern Ireland, Catholics and Protestants, kill one another, just as the Norsemen of the sagas, with their ferocious ethic of revenge, killed one another. The poem envisages a propitiatory and assuaging rite which may satisfy all those in the North who 'pine for ceremony, / customary rhythms' (with its ironic echo of Yeats in 'A Prayer for my Daughter' – 'Hcw but in custom and in ceremony / Are innocence and beauty born?'). Of its nature, this has to be a rite which transcends the Christian rituals of the religions in whose name this 'neighbourly murder' is committed: Heaney is perhaps implicating the Catholicism of his childhood in such guilt when he imagines his relations' hands 'shackled in rosary beads', the religion as a kind of enslavement.

The extraordinary procession imagined in the second section of 'Funeral Rites' goes beyond, or below, Christianity, as Heaney wills a reconciliatory funeral rite into being:

> I would restore
>
> the great chambers of Boyne,
> prepare a sepulchre
> under the cupmarked stones. . . .
>
> Quiet as a serpent
> in its grassy boulevard

> the procession drags its tail
> out of the Gap of the North
> as its head already enters
> the megalithic doorway.

In his book *The Making of the Reader*, David Trotter
has written very interestingly about Heaney's use of
the modal auxiliary 'would' in this passage, pointing
out that it moves away from the simply commemorat-
ive sense of typical earlier instances in the work ('I
would fill jampotfuls . . .' in 'Death of a Naturalist', for
instance) towards a 'fiercer optative mood'; and cer-
tainly the visionary grandeur of the lines is impelled
by the solemn desire in Heaney's tone. The Boyne,
scene of the victory in 1690 still celebrated annually by
Ulster Loyalists, is commemorated here not as the
source of sectarian division, but as the site of those
prehistoric burial chambers at Newgrange: the divisions
of the present, therefore, are healed in a rite which
insists on the common ground shared, in the North, by
both Catholic and Protestant. It is a rite in which the
'whole country' can join; and this poem is the major
instance in Heaney's work where 'we' and 'our' define a
community larger than that of the Catholics of the
North.

The reconciliatory possibility is imaged, finally, in
an allusion to that pacific moment in the Icelandic
Njal's Saga when, uniquely, there seems to be a brief
respite in the revenge cycle catalogued remorselessly
in the rest of the tale. Gunnar, a victim (although
previously an ardent perpetrator) of violence, is
imagined 'joyful' in death, although 'unavenged'. The
poem's hope is that those 'disposed like Gunnar' during
the imagined funeral rites on the Boyne may remain
similarly 'unavenged' by their mourners, who are sud-
denly turned into Norsemen when they drive back not

past Strangford and Carlingford, but past 'Strang and Carling fjords' – a reminder that the Vikings have left their names, as they might be thought to have left their ethical code, in the North of Ireland.

'Funeral Rites', however, is only, to use Trotter's word, 'optative': it urgently desires an end to the terrible cycle, but it can imagine such a thing only in a mythologized visionary realm. The four lights burning in Gunnar's burial chamber are only a very flickering illumination in the darkness of the other Viking poems in the book, whose discovery of persistence and continuity obliterates much sense of optimism about a possible future. And when, in 'Viking Dublin', Heaney prays to these butchering forefathers, it is to insist on the repetitions of Irish history:

> Old fathers, be with us.
> Old cunning assessors
> of feuds and of sites
> for ambush or town.

The prayer recalls Stephen's prayer to Daedalus at the end of *A Portrait of the Artist*, 'Old father, old artificer, stand me now and ever in good stead', and Yeats's prefatory poem to *Responsibilities*, 'Pardon, old fathers ... / Merchant and scholar who have left me blood'. Heaney's location of the Irish paternity theme in this Viking source is exhausted and despairing; it is at one, in 'Viking Dublin', with the devastating pun which – prompted by Jimmy Farrell in Synge's *Playboy of the Western World* – sees the 'cobbled quays' of Dublin as 'the skull-capped ground'.

'Bone Dreams', which takes its images not from the Viking, but from the English invasions of Ireland, effects a kind of transition between the Viking poems and the bog poems of Part I. Beginning in an act of anger and aggression, when Heaney pitches a bone at England in 'the sling of mind', the sequence moves to its close in metaphors of lovemaking which imagine the English language and landscape as a woman's body. These sections of the poem, IV and V, are as strange as anything Heaney has written, fascinatedly creating a sexual philology and topography; they owe something, perhaps, to Henry Moore's huge woman-landscape sculptures, and they are not entirely unlike some moments in the work of David Jones and of Heaney's contemporary, Michael Longley. They make the reaction to 'England' conveyed by 'Bone Dreams' a very complex one: anger, but also rich philological delight in its language, and an intimate imaginative infatuation with some of its landscapes most redolent of succeeding ages of human habitation (the prehistoric Giant of Cerne Abbas, priapic on the South Downs, evoked in IV; Hadrian's Wall; Maiden Castle). The poem as a whole, indeed, transforms its initial act of aggression into a final tenderness, as Heaney touches, for the first time, the 'small distant Pennines' of a mole's shoulders in Devon – the mole native to England's 'strange fields', but unknown in Ireland.

'Bone Dreams' also sounds that note of sexuality, of carnality, sustained by the bog poems which follow. The sexual is implicit in the material itself, since the bog people were sacrificed in vegetation rites, and the Tollund man in *Wintering Out* is a 'bridegroom to the goddess'. A wholly new element is introduced, however, when, as happens in several of the bog poems, we are made aware of a male poet gazing on, and responding to, female victims. Marked by the unease of their own reactions, these poems nevertheless involve themselves in dangerous emotions. Familiarity should not dull their edge of scandal: they are poems whose artfulness operates in the vicinity not only of voyeurism, but

[112]

of necrophilia and of an attraction to the bodily marks of pain. They combine, as Eliot said the 'auditory imagination' combined, 'the most ancient and the most civilized mentality'.

Their usefulness in the construction of a myth for Northern Ireland, however, is in their confounding of the sexual and the political. This operates in a quasi-allegorical way in the first two poems, 'Come to the Bower' and 'Bog Queen', where the bog woman is not one of Glob's Jutland bodies, but the first properly documented body ever taken from a bog, that of the 'queen' discovered on the Moira estate, about twenty miles south of Belfast, in 1781. The fact that this was an Irish bog preservation, presumed to be the skeleton of a Danish Viking, is clearly important to Heaney, since it offers him a genuinely historical, not merely an imaginative, connection between Ireland and Jutland.

In 'Come to the Bower', the 'bower' is the arbour sacred to Nerthus in which the body is sacrificed; it is the 'boudoir' which generates the poem's sexual meta-phors, as the 'I' (both Heaney in imagination, and the actual discoverer of the skeleton, I presume) 'unpins' and 'unwraps' the body, reaching towards the 'Venus bone'; and it is also the 'bower' of Ireland itself, that bower in the popular Republican song whose title Heaney has taken for his poem. In that song, the 'tradition of Irish political martyrdom' which he be-lieves, he tells us in 'Feeling into Words', shares an 'archetypal pattern' with the religion of Nerthus is given one of its most bloodily mystical expressions (the soil of its bower is 'sanctified with the blood' of the dead); and Heaney's poem proposes its allegory in something of the way 'A New Song' in *Wintering Out* does: when 'spring water / Starts to rise around her', it is possibly the stirring of revolution (the Easter Rising?), and when the poem's 'I' reaches towards the 'bullion / Of her Venus bone', it is a gesture similar, perhaps, to that more specifically allegorical act of sexual-imperialist plunder in 'Act of Union'.

'Bog Queen' itself, in one of Heaney's strangest female monologues, pursues the allegory. The specific circumstances of the Moira bog woman (recovered from the bog after 'a peer's wife' – Lady Moira – had bribed the estate-worker who discovered her) assume a range of implications which make her a kind of Kathleen ni Houlihan, a kind of Mother Ireland. She is placed (like Heaney's own first home) 'between turf-face and demesne wall'; her native authority, symbolized by her diadem, is gradually undermined 'like the bearings of history'; her hair is 'robbed'. The poem is, on one level, an extremely accurate account of the processes of her decay, of the body being reclaimed by, and turning into, the land itself; but the implications raise the bog queen to the status of a symbol for disaffected native resentment, biding its time underground ('I lay waiting . . .', spoken twice, in promise or threat), or prospering in the womb of the land until – 'the birth-cord / of bog' cut – it rises again into the light. The poem may be a version, in fact, of the 'sleeping giant' theme subsequently criticized in 'Hercules and Antaeus'.

Having suggested, in these implied allegories, a connection between bog bodies and Irish Republicanism, Heaney goes on, in the next two poems of the sequence, 'The Grauballe Man' and 'Punishment', to make direct analogies between these bog people and the contemporary victims of sectarian atrocity: 'The Grauballe Man' concludes with an evocation of 'each hooded victim, / slashed and dumped', and 'Punishment' imagines the Windeby bog girl of Glob's account, possibly punished for adultery, as the 'sister' of those Catholic girls tarred and feathered in Northern Ireland during the early 1970s as a punishment for 'going with' British soldiers.

Both poems explore Heaney's own perturbedly ambiguous responses. 'The Grauballe Man' admits the ways in which such instances of suffering can be turned to artistic account, as the successive photographs in Glob's book, which show the man being gradually removed from the bog, suggest not death but childbirth, and make the victim almost an icon, his corpse a 'vivid cast', his body having its 'opaque repose'. Even the wound in his 'slashed throat' is 'cured' – meaning 'preserved', of course, but with the inevitable association of 'healed' hovering over it. The precision and meticulousness of Heaney's metaphors are perhaps a similar appropriation of the human victim to the poem's own form and order. In the final stanza, however, the victim – the man himself, then, and each similar murdered corpse, now – sickeningly thuds out of his artistic 'repose' into the brute, realistic horror of 'slashed' and 'dumped'. The man's 'actual weight' falls as a rebuke to Heaney's own mythologizing tendency: rarely has the word 'actual' carried so much weight (unless it is in the seventh of Heaney's own 'Glanmore Sonnets' – 'It was marvellous / And actual'), as it insists that murder, then as now, happens in 'act', not 'art', in deed, not word. Who will say 'corpse' to his vivid cast? This very poem itself.

In 'Punishment', the ambiguity of Heaney's response is a more specifically political one, as the almost-love poem ('My poor scapegoat, / / I almost love you'), with its tender empathies, releases its concluding identification and self-definition:

> I who have stood dumb
> when your betraying sisters,
> cauled in tar,
> wept by the railings,

> who would connive
> in civilized outrage
> yet understand the exact
> and tribal, intimate revenge.

These lines have given rise to critical debate about precisely what position in relation to IRA violence the poem is assuming: if the 'civilized outrage' is 'connivance', with that word's implication of the underhand and the conspiratorial, and the revenge is 'exact' – appropriate, correspondent to the crime – then presumably the 'understanding' is also a condoning. In his review of *North*, Conor Cruise O'Brien certainly thought so:

> It is the word 'exact' that hurts most: Seamus Heaney has so greatly earned the right to use this word that to see him use it as he does here opens up a sort of chasm. But then, of course, that is what he is about. The word 'exact' fits the situation as it is felt to be: and it is because it fits, and because other situations, among the rival population, turn on similarly oiled pivots, that hope succumbs. I have read many pessimistic analyses of 'Northern Ireland', but none that has the bleak conclusiveness of these poems.

Certainly the poem's business is to remind us, once again, of the persistence of atavistic emotions and responses in the North, and in Seamus Heaney himself as a Northern Catholic. It is the point of the myth of *North* that it should do this, and that, in doing this, it should criticize the shallowness and presumption of most rationalist, humanist responses. Nevertheless, Heaney's dumbness before the contemporary tarred-and-feathered 'sisters' is itself implicitly criticized by the poem's biblical allusions, which bring a third religion, Christianity, into the reckoning, along with the Iron Age territorial religion and the 'religion' of Irish Republicanism. When Heaney says he 'would have cast . . . / the stones of silence', the 'Little adulteress' of 'Punishment' acquires another 'sister', the woman taken in adultery in the eighth chapter of St John's gospel, where Christ tells the crowd gathered to stone her, 'He that is without sin among you, let him first cast a stone at her.' Nobody does, of course; but Heaney, like the others of his 'tribe', casts those equally blameworthy 'stones of silence' and dumbness.

The poem includes further, more subdued biblical references: the 'scapegoat' of Leviticus, which takes on the sins of the tribe and is driven into the wilderness, a usage applied to Christ in the Catholic liturgy; and the girl's 'numbered bones', which derive from one of the psalms also used of Christ in Catholic worship, 'They have pierced my hands and feet; they have numbered all my bones.' The chilling irony of these allusions is that they both judge this act of tribal revenge by the more merciful ethic enshrined in the biblical religion, while they also implicate that religion in precisely those sacrificial rituals which join Jutland and Irish Republicanism. The allusion to the woman taken in adultery, however, complicates the moral questions raised by the poem: if Heaney's dumbness is blameworthy, then neither 'connivance' nor 'understanding' can excuse it; and the poem's predominant emotion, an empathetic pity for the victim, confirms the self-judgement.

The poem which follows 'Punishment', 'Strange Fruit', might be thought to intensify this self-rebuke when the girl's blank eyes remain 'outstaring / What had begun to feel like reverence'. Her gaze is a rebuke to the poet intruding on her death; and the myth is humbled by the fact, shamed by the reality of the 'terrible', brutally treated human victim.

The final bog poem, 'Kinship', is a summarizing hymn to the bog, in which Heaney establishes his own intimacy with the terrain of bogland, reading out of its 'hieroglyphic' landscape his personal 'kinship' to the victims of Jutland. The poem's six sections exhibit different aspects of his relationship to the bog: his physical delight in it (I); his derivation of a history and a psychology from the word itself (one of the very few importations from Irish into English), which make the bog both the memory of the landscape and the 'outback of my mind' (II); his mythologizing of the bog by 'twin-ning' an old moss-covered turf-spade with the 'cloven oak-limb' representative of the goddess Nerthus (III); his imagining it as language or poem, which he and his work 'grew out of' (IV); his memory of helping a turf-cutter (his grandfather?) as a child, a section written in the heraldic, archaizing language of some of *Stations*, which makes the turf-cutter a mythologized 'god of the waggon' and the boy Heaney his cup-bearer (V); and, finally, an address to the Roman historian Tacitus, who wrote about Ireland in his *Agricola* and who, in the fortieth chapter of his *Germania*, describes the cult of the goddess Nerthus.

That chapter opens, in the phrase quoted by Heaney, 'In an island of the ocean is a holy grove . . .', and it is the source of Glob's speculations about the religion of the bog people. Heaney's poem imagines the present in the North of Ireland in terms of Roman imperial conquest: 'a desolate peace' is a version of Tacitus's remark that 'They make a desolation and call it peace', and the Roman 'legions' who 'stare / from the ramparts' are, presumably, the 'occupying' forces of the British Army. In a conclusion which, like that of 'Punishment', has proved controversial, Tacitus is invited to

Come back to this
'island of the ocean'
where nothing will suffice.
Read the inhumed faces

of casualty and victim;
report us fairly,
how we slaughter
for the common good

and shave the heads
of the notorious,
how the goddess swallows
our love and terror.

Edna Longley, in her essay on *North* in *The Art of Seamus Heaney*, has spoken of the 'astonishingly introverted Catholic and Nationalist terms' of this section of 'Kinship', and Blake Morrison, failing to find any 'civilized irony' in the phrase 'slaughter / for the common good', has said that Heaney's poetry here 'grants sectarian killing in Northern Ireland a historical respectability which it is not usually granted in day-to-day journalism'. However, although this poem certainly marks the most intimate conjunction in these bog poems between the brutal Nordic religion and modern Ireland (that 'goddess' is both Nerthus and Kathleen ni Houlihan), there surely is irony in the phrase. The country in which this slaughter is carried on is an island in which 'nothing will suffice' (Yeats had asked, in 'Easter 1916', 'O when may it suffice?', after warning that 'Too long a sacrifice / Can make a stone of the heart'); and this 'nothing' must include such slaughter. It will not 'suffice', will not be adequate to the end in view – particularly if the end in view is the 'common good'. To bring into causal connection the barbarity of 'slaughter' and the civility of that English translation of the Roman ideal of civility, the *res publica*, is indeed an irony, and one not necessarily directed only against the native practice: those legions who stare from the ramparts are also quite capable of slaughtering for the common good; they are, after all, the ones who, by Tacitus's own account, make a desolation and call it peace.

Some such civilized, or barbarous, irony informs those allegorical poems which draw Part I of *North* to a conclusion, 'Ocean's Love to Ireland' and 'Act of Union'. Both allegorize crucial moments in the making of that desolation – and therefore in the history of Ireland's relationship with England – in sexual terms. 'Ocean's Love to Ireland' (its title an echo of Walter Ralegh's long poem to Elizabeth, 'Ocean's Love to Cynthia') ingeniously draws on a passage from John Aubrey's life of Ralegh to transform that 'love' into a rape. The relevant passage from *Brief Lives* reads:

> He loved a wench well; and one time getting up one of the Mayds of Honour up against a tree in a wood ('twas his first Lady) who seemed at first boarding to be something fearful of her Honour, and modest, she cryed, sweet Sir Walter, what doe you me ask? Will you undoe me? Nay, sweet Sir Walter! Sweet Sir Walter! At last, as the danger and the pleasure at the same time grew higher, she cryed in the extasey, Swisser Swatter Swisser Swatter. She proved with child, and I doubt not but this Hero tooke care of them both, as also that the Product was more than an ordinary mortal.

Heaney's poem, imagining the maid backed by Ralegh to a tree 'As Ireland is backed to England', folds the Aubrey story around an evocation of the massacre at Smerwick in Co. Kerry in 1580, in which Ralegh was instrumental. A small Spanish-Catholic defence force sent by the Pope to the aid of the Irish was murdered

[120]

there after surrendering. The quotation in the poem's second section is taken from an account of the massacre dictated by the English commander, Lord Grey, to his secretary, the poet Edmund Spenser. In 'Ocean's Love to Ireland', then, Ireland is the maid 'ruined' by Ralegh's imperial, plundering rape, and forced to surrender her language to the 'Iambic drums' of these English poet-courtiers. This is a poem in which, it might be said, Ralegh and Spenser are caught in the act of slaughtering for the common good – or at least for the common good of those English colonists who dispossessed the rebel landholders after Smerwick.

'Act of Union' is almost as strangely inhabited a monologue as 'Bog Queen': if in that poem it is, in a sense, Ireland who speaks, here it is England. The Act of Union of the title is the parliamentary act of 1800 which was England's response to the 1798 rebellion, and which created, from 1 January 1801, the 'United Kingdom of Great Britain and Ireland'. The poem, carrying further the sexual-political topography of 'Bone Dreams', imagines the act as one of sexual congress between England and Ireland: England 'imperially / Male', Ireland the woman made pregnant with the child whose 'first movement' is now being recognized by its father. Whether this child is Northern Ireland itself, or the Loyalist presence in Northern Ireland, the poem clearly regards the Act of Union as initiating a process which 'Culminates inexorably' in the present Troubles – in this child whose 'parasitical / And ignorant little fists' are raised against both Ireland and England. The conclusion of the poem – revised from its original lengthier, more optimistic version (published in the *Listener*, 22 February 1973) – is hopeless and exhausted, the rhyme of 'pain' and 'again' insisting on the apparent endlessness of political suffering in Irish history:

[121]

                                No treaty
            I foresee will salve completely your tracked
            And stretchmarked body, the big pain
            That leaves you raw, like opened ground, again.

The ingenuity of the analogies and metaphors of the
concluding poems of Part I is consistent with the
genuinely extraordinary nature of its other poems,
particularly the bog poems, which are, literally, like
nothing else in the language. They *insist* themselves on
the reader in a way that the more orthodox 'declarative'
poems of Part II do not even attempt; and it has generally
been thought, as it has of *Wintering Out*, that, apart
from 'Exposure', Part II represents a falling-off of imag-
inative power. I myself feel this, although I would read
it as part of the deliberated programme for the structure
of *North* which I have already described: as Heaney
explained to Robert Druce, the poems of Part II are
'poems which in a sense *anybody* could write. . . .
They're just telling – one kind of telling.' The compen-
sation is that this 'telling' (about Heaney's own sense
of the relationships possible between poetry and the
public life in 'The Unacknowledged Legislator's Dream',
'Freedman' and 'Whatever You Say Say Nothing'; and,
in 'Singing School', about some of the cultural circum-
stances in his own biography which have conditioned
his 'singing') releases an unexpected experimentalism
in his work, and eventually provokes, in 'Exposure', one
of his finest poems.
    The experiment with fantasy in 'The Unacknowledged
Legislator's Dream' is interestingly uncharacteristic, in
a mode Heaney has not worked again. The poem – which
is, despite its lineation, in fact a prose-poem – could be
said to undermine Shelley's Romantic conception of the
poet as 'the unacknowledged legislator of the world'

with something more akin to Auden's disillusioned modernist insistence that 'in our time the unacknow-ledged legislators are the secret police'. The poem, indeed, is a kind of parable of how, in Auden's view, 'poetry makes nothing happen': in Heaney's fantasy, the poet-as-liberator is simply imprisoned by the secret policeman, and his heroically or ludicrously Tarzan-like act is rendered even more futile by the policeman's mild-mannered solicitude ('You'll be safer here, any-how'). In 'Freedman', however, poetry, if it is not morally heroic, does provide the means of release from the most defining marks of tribe and caste (imaged as the ashes on one's forehead – 'a light stipple of dust' – which made a Catholic automatically identifiable in Northern Ire-land on Ash Wednesdays); but the release is paid for with reproach – 'Now they will say I bite the hand that fed me.' And in Heaney's most 'public' poem, 'Whatever You Say Say Nothing', poetry, in the form of allusion and of Heaney's desire 'To lure the tribal shoals to epigram / And order', must contend with journalistic cliché (one way of saying nothing) and with 'The famous / / Northern reticence, the tight gag of place', those sly obliquities of inspection and scrutiny operated by both communities. Heaney himself ends up saying not nothing, but what he has said before – the dedicatory poem of *Wintering Out*, repeated now (with one small variation) as the final poem of this sequence.

If these poems indicate, in different ways, some of the poets Heaney has subsequently chosen not to be, 'Singing School' moves towards a definition, in 'Ex-posure', of the kind of poet he thinks he is. Debating again some of the issues which have informed many of the poems in *North* at some level – the rival claims of art and action, of poetry and political accountability – 'Exposure' does so in a way which makes it a singularly appropriate final poem for this bipartite book: by drawing together its two major modes, the 'symbolic' and the 'declarative'. It is a poem in which, as Heaney has himself said about Yeats's 'Long-Legged Fly', 'every element . . . is at once literal and symbolic'.

Written after Heaney's move away from Belfast to Wicklow in 1972, the poem hovers between different meanings of the word 'exposure': the greater openness to the elements of living again in a rural environment; confessional self-revelation; and the media publicity which the move occasioned. Literally self-questioning, it sets Heaney in his first Wicklow winter, anxiously meditating on his own motivation and moving towards a moment of declaration which keeps unease in the balance with self-justification. The literal December, however, which is in any case a correlative for the poet's state of mind, with its 'damp leaves, / Husks, the spent flukes of autumn', also produces those symbolically instructive voices of the rain which 'Mutter about let-downs and erosions' and yet recall 'The diamond absolutes'; and it produces too the possibility of that symbolic comet, which in fact Heaney has 'missed' by the poem's close.

The subtle translation of the literal into the symbolic is accompanied by an allusiveness which exposes the Heaney of 'Exposure' to the example of the great modern Russian poet, Osip Mandelstam – an exercise in the exemplary entirely appropriate to the culminating poem of a sequence which takes its title from Yeats's 'Sailing to Byzantium', 'Nor is there singing school but studying / Monuments of its own magnificence'. When Heaney has himself 'Imagining a hero / On some muddy compound, / His gift like a slingstone / Whirled for the desperate', he is perhaps crossing an image of an Irish political prisoner (on the 'compound' of an internment camp) with an image of Mandelstam in one of Stalin's camps, after he had written his anti-Stalinist 'Stalin Epigram' ('David had faced Goliath with eight stony couplets in his sling', Heaney says of this poem in the uncollected article, 'Osip and Nadezhda Mandelstam'). The 'Epigram' was one of Mandelstam's very few directly confrontational poems; his more usual way was similar to Heaney's in Part I of *North*, as Heaney explained to Caroline Walsh: 'His poetry didn't deal in any obvious way with political messages: it brought the sense of terror, oppression, suffering into images, into music.' And Heaney implicitly draws the analogy with Mandelstam when he has himself weighing his 'responsible *tristia*': *Tristia* was the title given by its editor to one of Mandelstam's books, written out of the experience of being exiled in Voronezh, and itself echoing the title of Ovid's *Tristia*, written during his exile from Rome. The analogy is pursued when Heaney refers to himself as an 'inner émigré': as Nadezhda Mandelstam, Osip's widow, tells us in her memoir, *Hope Against Hope*, both Mandelstam and Anna Akhmatova were branded 'internal émigrés' while still living in Moscow – émigrés, that is, from the assumptions of the Soviet regime ('a label which was to play an important part in their subsequent fate').

Heaney's analogy between his own voluntary and comfortable exile and Mandelstam's forced and terrible exile (which ended, eventually, in his death) would seem intolerably presumptuous and self-aggrandizing if the comparison did not provoke him into a saddened, but unapologetic, self-defence:

> I am neither internee nor informer;
> An inner émigré, grown long-haired
> And thoughtful, a wood-kerne
>
> Escaped from the massacre,
> Taking protective colouring
> From bole and bark, feeling
> Every wind that blows;

> Who, blowing up these sparks
> For their meagre heat, have missed
> The once-in-a-lifetime portent,
> The comet's pulsing rose.

The peculiarly negative affirmation of that is emphasized by the way it 'incubates a cadence' from Eliot (as Heaney has said, in 'The Fire i' the Flint', Eliot's 'Marina' incubates a cadence from Seneca) – the wan anti-heroics of Prufrock's 'No! I am not Prince Hamlet, nor was meant to be; / Am an attendant lord'.

But if the offered opportunity for action, or for the action of a particular kind of poem, has been 'missed', it is nevertheless an honourable position which has been won through to: Heaney may not be 'internee', the hero on a compound, but he is not 'informer' either, or betrayer. He is 'a wood-kerne', one of those rebels who, during the earlier course of Irish history, took to the woods, when defeated, to prepare for further resistance. The word implies that Heaney's 'exile', and the poetry he will compose during it, will not lack their political dimension; but the politics will take its 'protective colouring' from the obligations to art itself. In this sense, 'Exposure' defines the poems Heaney has actually written in *North* which, with their hard-earned 'diamond absolutes' – of poetic excellence and of public accountability – themselves constitute the 'weighing and weighing' of 'responsible *tristia*'.

V

Opened Ground:
Field Work (1979)

I suppose that the shift from *North* to *Field Work* is a shift
in trust: a learning to trust melody, to trust art as reality,
to trust artfulness as an affirmation and not to go into the
self-punishment so much. I distrust that attitude too, of
course. Those two volumes are negotiating with each other.

Seamus Heaney to Frank Kinahan, 1982

'I'm certain that up to *North*,' Seamus Heaney told John
Haffenden in 1979, 'that was one book; in a way it goes
together and grows together.' Turned inward in scrutiny
of the self, and of the culture which had produced the
self, the work from *Death of a Naturalist* to *North* had
established a relatively narrow range of images and
procedures as the characteristic Heaney territory, and
its predominant virtues were those of intensity, scrupu-
lousness and precision. The second part of *North*, how-
ever, gave notice of a desire to turn the almost morosely
self-entranced voice outwards in some more sociable
kind of address; and in several interviews, Heaney has
spoken of his attempt in *Field Work* to bring a sense of
his ordinary social self into his poetry. The abandonment
of the very short, clipped, curt line of *North*, in favour of
a return to the longer line of his earliest work, is regarded
as the entering into of a 'rhythmic contract' with an
audience, a formal guarantee that the poetry is intended
as communication as well as self-communication.

As its title, which suggests a collection of different

samples, implies, *Field Work* is certainly more relaxed in its structure than *North*, less concentratedly intent on its own coherence. It brings together poems in a variety of kinds – political poems, 'pastoral' poems, elegies, love or 'marriage' poems, and a translation. In place of the previous book's chastened, ascetic restraint, there is a relished sensuousness of natural imagery; and the self-communing, mythologized 'I' of *North* is replaced by a more genuinely personal personal pronoun, a more openly and intimately conversational self. In his interview with James Randall, Heaney remembers that he wrote to Brian Friel at the time that 'I no longer wanted a door into the dark, I wanted a door into the light . . . to be able to use the first person singular to mean *me* and my lifetime.'

The desire to write about the ordinary world, and the ordinary social self, was balanced in Heaney, however, by a strong sense of the ways in which the personal and domestic life can seem merely tedious or narcissistically presumptuous in contemporary poetry. He wanted to find a way, he told Frank Kinahan, 'to fortify the quotidian into a work'; and it was in the poetry of Robert Lowell that he discovered the most compelling exemplification of how such a 'fortification' might occur. Lowell's impact on Heaney is pervasive in *Field Work*. Occasionally this can be disconcerting, when he appears merely to have taken over a Lowellian mannerism: the adjectival run, for instance ('Acrid, brassy, genital, ejected', of bullets, in 'The Strand at Lough Beg'), or the oracular rhetorical question ('How perilous is it to choose / not to love the life we're shown?' in 'The Badgers'), or the plaintively intimate 'Remember our American wake?' in 'September Song', which seems to remember several similar queries in Lowell ('Remember our lists of birds?', 'Remember summer?', 'Remember standing with me in the dark, / escaping?').

These are undoubtedly debilitating moments, but they pale beside recognition of Heaney's more deeply assimilated Lowellian procedures, in which he has inherited a way of being 'braced' and 'profiled' (his words for Lowell in 'Full Face' in *Preoccupations*) in an autobiographical poem. In particular, Heaney has caught from Lowell that very artful combination of intent concentration and almost-inconsequentiality which, in a range of poems from *Life Studies* to *The Dolphin*, deflects confessional narcissism into an insouciant drama of self-perception.

The major poetic presence in *Field Work*, and in much of Heaney's subsequent work, is not Lowell, however, but Dante. He is present in the epigraph (from the *Purgatorio*) to 'The Strand at Lough Beg', and in that poem's haunting conclusion, where Heaney wipes his murdered cousin's face with dew and moss, as Virgil wipes Dante's face at the opening of the *Purgatorio* itself. He provides the witty conceit of 'An Afterwards', which sets Heaney in the ninth circle of the *Inferno*, for the domestic treachery of too great a devotion to his art. In 'Leavings', Thomas Cromwell, despoiler of the English monasteries, is similarly imagined in one of hell's circles, 'scalding on cobbles, / each one a broken statue's head'; and the opening line of 'September Song', 'In the middle of the way', is a version of the opening of the whole *Commedia*, '*Nel mezzo del cammin di nostra vita . . .*' Above all, Dante figures in the translation from Cantos 32 and 33 of the *Inferno* which Heaney calls 'Ugolino' and uses to bring *Field Work* to a conclusion.

Dante is important to Heaney in one straightforward, and in one perhaps surprising, way. *The Divine Comedy* is a series of encounters with the dead, who offer explanations of their fate and – if they are the luckier ones – advice, encouragement and instruction.

Heaney's book is full of encounters with his own dead. There are the violently dead of Northern Ireland: Colum McCartney, Heaney's second cousin, the victim of a random sectarian shooting in 1975; Sean Armstrong, a Belfast social worker whom Heaney had known at university, in 'A Postcard from North Antrim'; the victim in 'Casualty' (unnamed in the poem, but in fact a friend of Heaney's called Louis O'Neill); the 'murdered dead' and the 'violent shattered boy' of 'The Badgers'. Dead artists are also commemorated in the book's elegies: Sean O'Riada, the famous Irish composer who died at the age of 40 in 1971; Robert Lowell, who died in 1977; and Francis Ledwidge, the Irish poet killed fighting for England during the First World War. The Heaney of *Field Work* is haunted by these ghosts; and Dante is the greatest of all poetic communers with the dead.

In an interview with Denis O'Driscoll, however, Heaney has described a less obvious focus of his interest in Dante: in the *Commedia*, he says, 'the first person singular and the historical life, the circumstances of the time and the man's personal angers, are all part of the forcefulness of the utterance'. Heaney seems to be implying, then, that Dante, like Lowell, indicated to him something of the way in which the quotidian could be fortified into a work; and he may well have been impressed by Lowell's own versions of Dante, particularly the account of *Inferno* XV in *Near the Ocean*, 'Brunetto Latini'. Heaney's relationship with Dante reaches a further pitch of intensity in the 'Station Island' sequence of his next book.

In fact, the more personal voice of the poems which open *Field Work* is actually fortified by an awareness of the intimate relationship between the personal and the political or historical. In 'Oysters', the apparently innocent eating of a meal with friends, that paradigm of good-natured sociability, becomes the basis for a meditation on the difficulty of ever avoiding the larger contingencies. These oysters, 'Alive and violated', 'ripped and shucked and scattered', have their innocence violated too by knowledge of their place in the history of human taste. As the delicacy of the Romans, the oysters come tainted with the savagery of European imperialist history and with the pride of caste or class – the 'frond-lipped, brine-stung / Glut of privilege' which refuses Heaney any easy luxuriating in 'the cool of thatch and crockery'. His anger at the end of the poem is a resentment that such self-punitive knowledge keeps him from any untrammelled enjoyment of the meal, that such conscience prevents him from reposing his trust 'In the clear light, like poetry or freedom / Leaning in from sea'.

This 'light' is presumably the one Heaney told Friel he wanted a door into in *Field Work*, the light opposed to the 'dark' of Irish history and of his own self-scrutiny. It is a light 'like poetry', leaning in temptingly, invitingly, a poetry of the sea, not the land, transcending the diminishments of human history: poetry as alternative, as delight and consolation, as the free play of imagination. When Heaney eats the day 'Deliberately, that its tang / Might quicken me all into verb, pure verb', it is an impatient response to this cajoling invitation: being quickened into verb will remove him, once and for all, from the enclosing, static nouns of earth and myth and placename. Yet the repose of such unfettered imagination, however deeply it is desired (and 'Oysters' makes it seem sweetly desirable), cannot be attained by mere effort of will. After such knowledge, light can never be so easily 'clear' again.

Indeed, as if to emphasize the equivocal nature of this meal with which *Field Work* opens, the book closes with the eating of a kind of meal too. In 'Ugolino',

Ugolino gnaws at Archbishop Roger's head in a grotesque parody of a meal: he and his sons and grandsons had been starved to death by Roger, and this is the eternal punishment fitting the crime. In translating Dante here, Heaney introduces a metaphor and a simile not in the original, which point up the comparison between this hideous act and the eating of a meal: the 'sweet fruit of the brain', and the head 'As if it were some spattered carnal melon'. The picture of enemies eternally locked in a literal enactment of 'devouring hatred' has, of course, its relevance to Northern Ireland, just as dying of hunger has its reverberations in Irish history and politics. The 'clear light' of the poetry desired in 'Oysters' is in fact darkened frequently in *Field Work* by such shadows from the old conflict; and the poems which follow 'Oysters', 'Triptych' and 'The Toome Road', are, once again, consumed by it.

Both poems make use of an oracular, vatic, quasi-Yeatsian rhetoric. It is a manner which can be used only very sparingly by a contemporary poet if it is not to seem presumptuously overweening; but in 'Triptych' it gives a persuasively magisterial and authoritative air to the poem's pained view of the present state of Ireland – now, for the first time in Heaney's work, the South with its mercenary acquisitiveness, as well as the North and its sectarian violence.

The panels of this triptych propose, very tentatively, images of some kind of comprehension, or consolation, or simple endurance. In 'After a Killing' (written after the murder of the British ambassador to Ireland, Christopher Ewart-Biggs, in July 1976), the 'small-eyed survivor flowers', the 'Broad window light' and the young girl's gift of vegetables are literal, if symbolically resonant, natural compensations for the obdurate persistence of the images of violence and desolation with which the poem opens. In 'Sybil', the girl – who had been, glancingly, a kind of Ceres-figure in 'After a Killing' – is more deliberately mythologized, as she utters her sybilline prophecy, with its faint hope of 'forgiveness'. The extraordinary image of new life returning to the 'helmeted and bleeding tree' may, it has been suggested, owe something to the trees in the underworld of Virgil's *Aeneid*, and to the frontispiece drawing by David Jones for his poem about the First World War, *In Parenthesis*. As these possible influences suggest, Heaney has risen to his occasion here, drawing together the grandiose and the tenderly human (those 'buds like infants' fists'), to create a powerful sense of alternative possibility, of the releasing hope of some kind of fulfilment.

Nevertheless, the hope is, realistically, wearily conditional, abrupted before the clause in which it is uttered can become a sentence:

> Unless forgiveness finds its nerve and voice,
> Unless the helmeted and bleeding tree
> Can green and open buds like infants' fists
> And the fouled magma incubate
>
> Bright nymphs. . . .

Those Lowellian dots of omission are the voice failing to find its nerve; and this makes the tentative optimism a sudden brief irruption into a poem which otherwise throws its attention back onto the prophecy of what will happen without such 'forgiveness' – the change of human form into some canine or insectile alternative – and forward to the evocation of the actual Irish present, in which the European profit motive is unidealistically pursued.

Heaney's 'bleeding tree', as an emblem for such an Ireland, may be an implicit revision of Yeats's magnificent unitary, harmonizing symbol in 'Among School

Children', the 'chestnut tree, great-rooted blossomer'; and the Yeatsian rhetoric to which 'Triptych' can rise is not allowed its head. The language of visionary possibility must engage the stubborn compunctions of the actual. Which makes it entirely appropriate that the sybil's final line is an ironic and despairing allusion to Shakespeare: 'Our island is full of comfortless noises' remembers, and reverses, Caliban in *The Tempest* – 'Be not afeard: the isle is full of noises, / Sounds and sweet airs, that give delight, and hurt not' – by remembering too that, when Gloucester's eyes are put out in *Lear*, he is left 'all dark and comfortless'.

The third poem of 'Triptych', 'At the Water's Edge', sets Heaney amid the ancient Christian remains on the islands of Lough Beg, longing for the humbling postures of Christian penitence. But the religion (a religion which recommends 'forgiveness', of course) offers only 'silence', its holy-water stoup now only 'for rain water'; and the whole of 'Triptych' collapses back out of any visionary or religious possibility, into the 'irrevocable' political fact: the British Army helicopter 'shadowing' the march at Newry which followed as a protest against Bloody Sunday.

That march is 'our march', and they are 'my roads' which Heaney drives down when he meets the armoured convoy in 'The Toome Road'. The possessives are the signal of the outraged native challenge to the colonizing aggressor. Indeed, the British soldiers become, briefly, continuous with the forces of the Roman imperium evoked in 'Oysters', when they are anachronistically addressed as 'charioteers'. Against their presumption, Heaney oracularly insists on the sustaining, 'vibrant' presence of 'The invisible, untoppled omphalos'. This is, I take it, the navel of nationalist Irish feeling, maintaining on the road to Toome (with its 1798 associations) its persistent, defiant opposition to the colonial power; and Heaney deliberately assumes, in the poem, a representative role as the articulator of such feeling: 'I had rights-of-way, fields, cattle in my keeping'.

'The Toome Road', 'Triptych', the implied allegory of 'Ugolino', and the Northern Ireland elegies ensure that, for all its poems of the personal life, *Field Work* retains a large political resonance; and that, for all its trust in the healing and consolatory affirmations of the artistic act, and the married life, it remains uncomplacently open to the urgencies of its historical moment, and responsively alert to the world beyond poem and home.

The elegies for artists in *Field Work* imply lessons for Heaney's own art: O'Riada's joining of a sophisticated international musical culture with native Irish folk melody (suggested by his conducting 'like a drover with an ashplant / herding them south'), and its political ramifications – the composer as 'our jacobite, / . . . our young pretender'; Robert Lowell's promulgation of 'art's / deliberate, peremptory / love and arrogance'; Francis Ledwidge's acting as 'our dead enigma' in whom 'all the strains / Criss-cross in useless equilibrium' – the implication being, I presume, that similar strains in Heaney, sixty years later, can be made to 'criss-cross' more usefully. The poems have their interest, in that they mark a particular stage in Heaney's self-consciousness as an artist, but they seem too deliberately willed. The Lowell elegy in particular is altogether too 'arrogantly' knowing when it sets Heaney and Lowell together 'under the full bay tree' in Glanmore ('My sweet, who wears the bays . . .?', Heaney will ask in 'An Afterwards', where such arrogance earns its infernal rebuke). Where there is leisure for ambition there is, perhaps, too little grief.

The elegies for dead friends are another matter. The immediacy of Heaney's sympathy forces him, for the first time in his work, to confront directly – as he did not in the mythologized obliquities of *North* – the actual, realistic circumstances of sectarian murder. Colum McCartney is blessed, at the end of 'The Strand at Lough Beg', with a Dantean asperging, but he is also imagined 'with blood and roadside muck in your hair and eyes'; and before Heaney can plait those 'green scapulars' for his shroud (patriotic? resurrectionary? pastoral-elegiac?), he must lift the actual weight of the Irish countryman 'under the arms'. Sean Armstrong is urged, in the banter of desperation, to 'Get up from your blood on the floor' in 'A Postcard from North Antrim'. And Louis O'Neill in 'Casualty' is particularized in the moment of being blown to pieces, 'Remorse fused with terror / In his still knowable face' – that 'still knowable' insisting not only on what will become of his face a split-second later, but also on how he survives, now, in Heaney's memory and in this commemorative poem.

In the context of these specific deaths, Heaney is also compelled to confront his own evolving responses to the North. In 'The Strand at Lough Beg', this takes the form of a rueful acknowledgement of his family's incapacity for facing some of the violent realities of sectarianism – 'For you and yours and yours and mine fought shy, / Spoke an old language of conspirators / And could not crack the whip or seize the day.' The attitude is probed no further, but the poem makes it clear that McCartney has been killed by those who have cracked their whip and seized their day. When McCartney's ghost subsequently appears to Heaney in 'Station Island', it is to complain bitterly that Heaney's beautiful Dantean close to 'The Strand at Lough Beg' is a continuance in literature of such family incapacity: 'You confused

[136]

evasion and artistic tact . . . / and saccharined my death with morning dew'.

In 'Casualty', the finest of these elegies, Louis O'Neill has been killed because he has broken an IRA curfew after Bloody Sunday: he has been blown up in the reprisal bombing of a Protestant pub, to which he has gone drinking as an habitual and instinctive drive of his nature. As well as being a perfectly judged elegy for O'Neill, deftly evoking the quality of the man and his life, and genuinely grieved, 'Casualty' is also a meditation on the ethics of betraying 'our tribe's complicity', the complex loyalties of a Northern Catholic.

The poem is ironically written in the same metre as Yeats's 'The Fisherman', that poem which conjures from the Celtic Twilight an idealized West of Ireland peasant as the perfect, if unlikely, dedicatee of Yeats's work. O'Neill is a fisherman too, but a rather less idealized one, 'dole-kept'; and, knowing Heaney only in the pub and on the boat, he finds that 'other life' of poetry 'Incomprehensible', although he is curious. 'Casualty', nevertheless, brings Heaney's two lives together when it brings O'Neill – uncondescendingly – into this poem, the fisherman's 'turned back' watched by the poet's 'tentative art'. The closing lines of 'Casualty' join the fisherman's lines to the poet's lines in the word 'rhythm':

> As you find a rhythm
> Working you, slow mile by mile,
> Into your proper haunt
> Somewhere, well out, beyond . . .
>
> Dawn-sniffing revenant,
> Plodder through midnight rain,
> Question me again.

The 'question' is one which Heaney's meditation on O'Neill's fate has earlier made him ask himself – 'How culpable was he / That last night when he broke / Our tribe's complicity?' When O'Neill's fishing and Heaney's poetry are joined in these concluding lines, their mutual lonely 'beyondness' takes them 'well out' from that image of community, the 'common funeral' of the thirteen dead of Bloody Sunday, which occupies the central section of 'Casualty'. The terms of that description suggest constriction and the infantile –

> The common funeral
> Unrolled its swaddling band,
> Lapping, tightening
> Till we were braced and bound
> Like brothers in a ring.

– whereas the concluding evocation of O'Neill and Heaney sharing the boat is light with release: 'I tasted freedom with him' ('like poetry or freedom / Leaning in from sea', we remember, in 'Oysters').

Allowing his own former certainties to be questioned by the fisherman in this way may be regarded as an important point of growth in Heaney's work. The apparently confident analogies between poetry and rural crafts in the earlier work, which 'bound' the poet to the community, have been replaced, in the analogy of 'Casualty', by something much edgier, more uncertain, more 'tentative': one of the community's skills, as it is practised by the strong-willed O'Neill, offers a lesson in questioning the community's own values and presumptions. Heaney's invitation to O'Neill to 'Question me again' may be regarded as initiating the elaborate self-questioning of 'Station Island'.

The bibliography of an article on Seamus Heaney in a literary journal in 1970 credits him, bizarrely, with a book called *The Development of the Sacramentality of Marriage from Anselm of Laon to Thomas Aquinas*.

Perhaps the bibliographer had sybilline powers of prophecy, however, because the love poems or, as Heaney has called them, the 'marriage poems', which he was to publish in *Field Work* are some of the most outstanding celebrations of uxoriousness in modern poetry. Not, perhaps, that this is to say a great deal, since uxoriousness is a condition celebrated rarely enough in any poetry, ever. No doubt poets have been uxorious; but they have not much made it register, as lived experience, within their poetry. Some instances of the kind are notoriously embarrassing – Eliot's 'A Dedication to my Wife', for instance; and the best poems of marriage I know are either addressed to a dead wife (from Henry King's 'Exequy', to Montale's *Xenia*), or they are poems of a deeply troubled marriage (Lowell's *For Lizzie and Harriet* and *The Dolphin*) or they are both (Hardy's poems of 1912–13). But, even if there is little direct competition, Heaney's achievement in these poems is remarkable: he has managed a poetry of ordinary domestic happiness, of the dailiness and continuity of married love, which entirely lacks sentimentality or self-satisfaction.

They are restrained from such dangers partly by the fact that they do not disguise the difficulties (not, perhaps, that anyone remembering 'Summer Home' from *Wintering Out* is likely to need much reminding of them). In 'High Summer', there is the teething child who cries 'inconsolably' at night; in 'Polder', there are 'the sudden outburst and the squalls' of a domestic row; and in 'The Otter', marriage as an evolving process is figured tactfully and gracefully in the correlative of the changing weathers of Tuscany:

> The mellowed clarities, the grape-deep air
> Thinned and disappointed.

Thank God for the slow loadening,
When I hold you now
We are close and deep
As the atmosphere on water.

In 'An Afterwards', the constant accommodations to be
made between domestic obligation and responsibility to
one's art are imaged in the conceit which renders
Ugolino's punishment of Roger comically bathetic,
depicting the hell of poets concerned only with the 'bays'
of critical renown as 'a rabid egotistical daisy-chain'.
For all the poem's affectionate comedy, though, the
wife's question, with its heart-sinking enjambment, is
very poignant, sadly rebuking the poet's self-absorption:

'Why could you not have, oftener, in our years

Unclenched, and come down laughing from your room
And walked the twilight with me and your children –
Like that one evening of elder bloom
And hay, when the wild roses were fading?'

She lets him off the hook, nevertheless, for his 'kind, /
Indifferent, faults-on-both-sides tact'; but he is not so
lightly dismissed in 'A Dream of Jealousy'. Even if the
opportunity for jealousy is being given only in 'a
dream' in that poem, there is nevertheless no remedy
for the hurt it causes. Neither in the order of aesthetics
('these verses', with their beguiling allurements, in-
cluding a submerged reference to Manet's *Déjeuner sur
l'Herbe*), nor in the moral order ('my prudence'), is
there balm for the woman's 'wounded stare': it survives
the sonnet's apology, as the bog woman's stare sur-
vives 'Strange Fruit'.

By admitting the difficulties, then, these poems re-
fuse to idealize human love, as they also refuse to
idealize the human body. In a series of extraordinary
zoomorphizing analogies (perhaps also partly indebted

to Robert Lowell, whose work is full of animal and piscine life, even though he hardly ever writes explicitly about animals or fish), the woman is an otter, a skunk, and a sandmartin's nest. Heaney is also ironically self-deprecating: he is 'tense as a voyeur' in 'The Skunk'; he is the sandmartin desperate for the 'occlusion' of the nest in 'Homecomings'; and he is 'like an old willow' in the lovely 'Polder'. The analogies and the anti-romantic attitudes insist on the embodied nature of love, and on the body's inevitable imperfections. As in the remarkable erotic ritual which closes the 'Field Work' sequence itself, however – that sequence which gazes on the imperfection of vaccination marks stretched on arm and thigh – these are imperfections which, through the intent devotion of sexual love, may be 'stained, stained / to perfection'. In these poems, despite the sometimes conflicting claims of art and home, there is no question of the impossible and inhuman Yeatsian choice between 'perfection of the life or of the work'. Being 'stained to perfection' is a latter-day *felix culpa*, the oxymoronic conjunction of nature and art, of the human body and the human will, which can create if not the 'sacramentality', then certainly the 'anointing' (the word of 'Field Work') of a happy marriage.

But this is to overstate what these poems gently understate, nowhere more than in what seems to me the most perfect of them, 'The Skunk'. Its title, and the glimpse of Heaney as voyeur, obviously recall Lowell's 'Skunk Hour'; but the mood of that disconsolate, desolating poem is as far from Heaney's as it is possible to imagine. Lowell's 'skunk hour' is a time of intense, infernal isolation ('I myself am hell, / nobody's here'), whereas Heaney's skunk acts as an emblem for the way his aloneness is a mere physical accident, suffused with his wife's presence when, away from her in California, he writes her a love letter. The skunk – 'intent and glamorous', 'ordinary, mysterious', 'mythologized, demythologized' – takes on the 'oxymoronic' qualities of the woman much known and much missed: so that the risky comparison, made while he is with her again in their bedroom, is charged with affection and intimacy, turning a faintly ridiculous human posture into an unconscious erotic invitation:

> It all came back to me last night, stirred
> By the sootfall of your things at bedtime,
> Your head-down, tail-up hunt in a bottom drawer
> For the black plunge-line nightdress.

The unromanticizing exactitude of the poem, its trustful certainty that it cannot put a foot wrong, or strike a false note, is clinched by the word 'sootfall'. A lovely nonce word (like Eliot's 'smokefall' in 'Burnt Norton'), it is beautifully accurate in the way it listens to the clothes falling to the bedroom floor, but it also remembers that the clothes are, like all clothes falling from a human body at bedtime, dirty. To be 'stirred' by such a 'sootfall' is to bear witness to the ordinary mysteriousness of a marriage; and 'The Skunk' is a tender, loving comedy of the consolations of the habitual, not least in the quietly uninsistent way it makes it plain that the skunk-like hunt for that suggestive 'black plunge-line nightdress' is quite unnecessary.

'The Skunk' is characteristic of these marriage poems, which are one of the highest points of Heaney's career: tender without being cosy, personal without being embarrassingly self-revealing. They are poems of a deeply disinterested maturity, managing an intensely difficult tone: honest, and quite without self-regard.

The sequence of ten 'Glanmore Sonnets' which lies physically at the centre of *Field Work* does indeed, as the book's original blurb proclaimed, 'concentrate themes apparent elsewhere in the book'; but the high art of these poems is all in how the concentration is managed. The fact that Heaney chooses to write a sonnet sequence at this stage of his career, after the disruption of the lyric in *North*, is in one way his most open acknowledgement in *Field Work* of an indebtedness to the English lyric tradition (Thomas Wyatt, the first English sonneteer, is alluded to in the tenth sonnet); but it perhaps fuses that allegiance with a further acknowledgement to Patrick Kavanagh. His sonnet sequence, 'Temptation in Harvest', with its delicate register of the rural world of his native Co. Monaghan, may have given Heaney a hint for the Glanmore sequence: in his essay on Kavanagh in *Preoccupations*, 'From Monaghan to the Grand Canal', Heaney says that the last sections of 'Temptation in Harvest' 'beautifully and wistfully annotate . . . his move to Dublin in 1939'. The 'Glanmore Sonnets' also annotate a move, from Belfast to Glanmore, close to Dublin, a move out of an urban environment back into a rural one, in some ways close to Heaney's own first world. On one level then, the sonnets are what Kavanagh's sequence is, though to my mind much more successfully: a sensuously exact evocation of living eye-level close to the processes and seasons of the natural world, its animal life and its vegetation. Unlike Kavanagh, however, Heaney discovers there a new point of confirmation and resolution, a firmer ground.

'Ground' is the word which ends the first line of the first sonnet, in the phrase 'opened ground'. This glances back at 'Act of Union' in *North*, where the 'opened ground' is the raw wound left on Ireland by England's siring on her of the North. In the 'Glanmore Sonnets', the phrase is deliberately translated out of that historical agony into the realm of aesthetics: the 'ground' is now that of poetry itself. The 'vowels ploughed into other' of that opening line are perhaps the vowels of Irish speech worked into the otherness of the English iambic line, and they may also be the words of the poem itself, which must be worked into the otherness of the actual world before they can carry any moral weight.

This intertwining of language and reality recurs, in different ways, during the sequence. It is made plainest, in these opening sonnets, in the line, 'Each verse returning like the plough turned round', a simile suggested by the derivation of 'verse' from the Latin *versus*, which meant both a line of verse and the turn made by the ploughshare from one furrow into the next. This original linguistic juncture between agriculture and culture is at one with the identifications Heaney makes between nature and poetry: an evening 'all crepuscular and iambic', and a wind which 'Is cadences'. This delighted, sensuous merging of facts of nature and facts of culture may derive its originating impulse from a poem of Mandelstam's, no. 62, in the W. S. Merwin and Clarence Brown translation of 1973. It is a poem which the 'Glanmore Sonnets' could be said secretly to nurture and address:

> Orioles in the woods: length of vowels alone
> makes the metre of the classic lines. No more
> than once a year, though, nature pours out
> the full-drawn length, the verse of Homer.
>
> This day yawns like a caesura: a lull
> beginning in the morning, difficult, going on and on:
> the grazing oxen, the golden languor powerless
> to call out of the reed the riches of one whole note.

If Mandelstam is a hidden presence in the sequence, other writers are there too, in varying degrees of visibility, in allusions which make the literary a mode of the perceiving consciousness in these poems. Boris Pasternak's 'Hamlet', the first of the *Doctor Zhivago* poems, ends with a Russian proverb which Lowell translates, in *Imitations*, 'To live a life is not to cross a field'; and Heaney's opening sonnet remembers this when it says of the relaxed ease of the Glanmore life, 'Now the good life could be to cross a field'. Wyatt, as I have noted, is alluded to in the tenth sonnet, where the tender eroticism of Heaney's 'first night' with his wife is tenderly allied to one of the most tenderly erotic moments in the whole of English poetry, in Wyatt's 'They flee from me':

> When her lose gowne from her shoulders did fall,
> And she me caught in her armes long and small;
> Therewithall sweetly did me kysse,
> And softly saide, *dere hert, howe like you this?*

More glancingly, Joyce is alluded to in the 'inwit' of IX (Stephen meditates in *Ulysses* on the medieval English phrase 'agenbite of inwit', remorse of conscience); Philip Sidney in 'What is my apology for poetry?' in X (he wrote a famous Renaissance treatise called the *Apology for Poetry*); and Shakespeare, also in X, with the eloping lovers Lorenzo and Jessica from *The Merchant of Venice* (Diarmuid and Grainne in the same sonnet are similar lovers, pursued in Gaelic mythology).

Above all, though, it is Wordsworth who shadows the sequence, as obviously present here as he is in *Death of a Naturalist*. In II, 'sensings, mountings from the hiding places' is Wordsworthian in its participial forms, and in its reference to 'the hiding places of my power' in *The Prelude*. In III, Heaney is about to make a direct comparison of his wife and himself, in their 'strange loneliness', to Dorothy and William in Rydal Mount, but the hyperbole is deflated by his wife's interrupting demurral. Sonnets IV, V and VI may also be thought Wordsworthian in the way they seek out moments analogous to *The Prelude*'s 'spots of time' – moments from Heaney's childhood which are witness to some sort of imaginative extension. In IV, the child misses the reputed 'iron tune' of the train when he puts his ear to the line, but the adult retrieves a poem from the memory. In V, the meditation on the tree associated with early sexual experience – in dialect the 'boortree', in 'proper' English the 'elderberry' – is offered as one instance of what has made this poet an 'etymologist of roots and graftings' in the 'tree' of language. And in VI the legendary story of 'the man who dared the ice' is an implied analogy from Heaney's childhood for the daring, attack, inspiration and impetuousness of a particular kind of poem, whose chanciness and risk are also 'a cold where things might crystallize or founder'.

That poem refers to 'the unsayable lights'; but these are all poems which manage to 'say' complex experiences, even while reminding us of the difficulty with which any experience struggles out of its 'hiding place' into the articulation of a poem. Made partly out of other poems, and gratefully allusive to them, the 'Glanmore Sonnets' are nevertheless directed out towards the world as well as inwards towards literature itself, seeking their ideal in a harmoniously reciprocal relationship between art and nature, language and experience. The sequence discovers its finest metaphor for these correspondences not in literary creation, but in sculpture, when, in II, Oisin Kelly is imagined 'hankering after stone / That connived with the chisel, as if the grain / Remembered what the mallet tapped to know.'

An understanding of these relationships, however, is not simply given, it must be slowly acquired; and this is why Glanmore is a 'hedge-school' in which Heaney can learn a voice that might 'continue, hold, dispel, appease'. The 'hedge-schools' were the only means the native Irish had of gaining an education during the period of the Penal Laws, and we can take it that what this voice must dispel and appease is, at least in part, the inheritance of a history of violence and repression (the original title of the sequence, for a limited edition, was in fact *Hedge School*). For all that the sonnets find their comforts in 'pastoral' calm, in literature, and in the achieved mutuality of marriage, these consolations are set in their fragility against insistent reminders of the world's pain. In VIII, the innocent sight of a magpie inspecting a sleeping horse summons to mind the 'armour and carrion' of a historical battlefield; in IX, a rat 'Sways on the briar like infected fruit', terrifying the poet's wife, and other rats killed in threshing leave their 'Blood on a pitch-fork, blood on chaff and hay'; and the final sonnet evokes a dream in which husband and wife lie down together and apart, in the attitude of death, as well as the embrace of sexual love.

In 'Yeats as an Example?' in *Preoccupations*, Heaney claims that, in Yeats's poems, 'the finally exemplary moments are those when [the] powerful artistic control is vulnerable to the pain or pathos of life itself'. The strength of the 'Glanmore Sonnets' is that, for all the control of their artistry, and the self-delight of their literariness, they never forget this vulnerability. I think of their most characteristic, as well as 'exemplary', moments, then, as the conclusions of sonnets VIII and X. Sonnet VIII:

> Do you remember that pension in *Les Landes*
> Where the old one rocked and rocked and rocked
> A mongol in her lap, to little songs?
> Come to me quick, I am upstairs shaking.
> My all of you birchwood in lightning.

The poignant memory of human suffering there is

countered with the urgent imperative of sexual desire, as if the one could occlude the other. It is the vulnerable desperation which registers most powerfully, however, in the phrase 'My all of you', which effects a grammatical conjunction (of his possessive adjective and her personal pronoun) responsively imitative of the sexual conjunction itself, in which he will be taken over, possessed, taken out of himself, like the wood devoured by lightning. That 'all' rivals, in the sheer force of its plenitude, some Joycean uses of the word: Bloom in 'Lestrygonians', for instance ('Perfume of embraces all him assailed. With hungered flesh obscurely, he mutely craved to adore'), or Joyce himself in a letter to Nora of 22 August 1909 ('Give yourself to me, dearest, all, all when we meet'). It also perhaps remembers the concluding line of 'Oysters', with its hope that the day's tang 'Might quicken me all into verb, pure verb'. It is the humbled expression of overwhelming need, as well as of irresistible desire.

And X, with its echo of Wyatt:

> And in that dream I dreamt – how like you this? –
> Our first night years ago in that hotel
> When you came with your deliberate kiss
> To raise us towards the lovely and painful
> Covenants of flesh; our separateness;
> The respite in our dewy dreaming faces.

'Deliberate' is a beautifully tactful word, drawing love, responsibility and inexperience into its net; and 'raise' similarly entraps both sexual tumescence and spiritual uplifting. 'Lovely and painful' is a telling paradox ('quickly, quickly, / Because O it was painful', Ted Hughes has it in 'A Childish Prank', his sexual myth in *Crow*), just as these are 'covenants' which leave husband and wife, nevertheless, in their 'separateness'.

The kind of art Heaney longs for in 'Oysters' is one in which his trust might 'repose'; but the saving grace of his own in the 'Glanmore Sonnets' is that it culminates not in the permanence of 'repose', but only in the temporary relief of 'respite', implying that all the covenants made by flesh – in art and in marriage alike – are, finally, vulnerable to 'the pain or pathos of life itself'.

There are several other important poems in *Field Work* which do not fall into the categories I have described here, but which contribute powerfully to the book's character. Two of them, 'The Singer's House' and 'The Harvest Bow', which are related in some ways, interestingly suggest one possible sense of the relationship between art and politics which Heaney has acquired in his artistic retreat.

Both oppose instances of some kind of artistic perfection – the folksinger's song; the harvest bow – to the depredations of human life and history, and both include an implicit benediction for the future of Ireland. 'The Singer's House' contains one of Heaney's saddest generalized reflections:

> What do we say any more
> to conjure the salt of our earth?
> So much comes and is gone
> that should be crystal and kept
>
> and amicable weathers
> that bring up the grain of things,
> their tang of season and store,
> are all the packing we'll get.

The song celebrated in the poem is one of the things that might be 'said' in response to the query of the opening lines there. With 'a hint of the clip of the pick', it brings the Scots/British saltmining culture of the Northern seaport Carrickfergus (about which there is a well-known Irish folksong) to the singer's 'house' in Gweebarra, the bay in Co. Donegal: it therefore implies a new harmony between North and South. When, later in the poem, the seals are imagined as 'drowned souls' drawn towards the singer's voice, they become emblems of some kind of muted hope and new possibility: that they might 'change shape' is an optimistic version of that metamorphosis so terrifyingly prophesied in 'Sybil' (where the changed form would be a 'saurian relapse', a reversion to a reptilian condition). Heaney's final peremptory address to the singer – 'Raise it again, man. We still believe what we hear' – is an affirmation of an art which, in the face of human loss and diminishment, still presumes to offer a model of pacific reconciliation.

Its presumption is, however, in the word of 'Casualty', 'tentative' in the face of the apparent ineradicability of Irish violence. The motto of the harvest bow, at the end of its celebratory poem, is also uninsistently subjunctive: the bow is a 'frail device', easily destroyed, and it is said that *The end of art is peace* 'could be' its motto. The way the motto speaks out of the bow, on behalf of its tongue-tied maker, Heaney's father, may remind us of that other inanimate speaker in English poetry, that 'foster-child of silence', the urn, in Keats's 'Ode on a Grecian Urn'; but any comparison reveals too how very cautious Heaney's bow is. The motto is offered not as discovery and advice ('Beauty is truth, truth beauty'), but as frail aspiration.

It is, nevertheless, a hope offered by the most benign aspects of the whole of Heaney's own rural inheritance: the 'spirit of the corn' at the end of the poem is an apotheosis of the patient, devoted effort of human agriculture. In this sense, the poem may even be considered a revision of 'Digging'. In that poem, Heaney's pen became an agricultural implement like his father's spade; in 'The Harvest Bow', Heaney's father plaits, in the bow, a paradigm of art. These same hands which plait the bow have also, however, 'lapped the spurs on a lifetime of game cocks', and the urgency of the poem's desire for 'peace' is not likely to slip into any sentimentalizing of the threats always offered to it. Perhaps the motto even warily acknowledges that, if the 'end' (the aim and fruit) of art is peace, then peace may also be the 'end' (the finish) of art, since so much great art, and certainly the art of this poet, has been nourished by so much that is not 'peace'.

Whether this is the case or not, it is certainly this realism which leads Heaney to conclude *Field Work* not with the kind of placatory and absolving gestures represented by 'The Harvest Bow' and 'The Singer's House', but with the violence of 'Ugolino'. This account of Dante has had a mixed reception, and Heaney does seem strangely to have missed some opportunities: 'And if you are not crying, you are hardhearted' is a flatly cautious rendering of Dante's great climactic *'e se non piangi, di che pianger suoli?'* which demands the verbal repetition, and the interrogative challenge, for its heartbreaking effect. But the concluding section of the translation is, I think, a marvellous account of Dante's invective against Pisa, making out of Dante's simply descriptive reference to the Italian city (*'bel paese la dove 'l sì suona'* / 'fair land where the *sì* is heard') a venomous sibillance which hides a snake in its grass: 'Pisa! Pisa, your sounds are like a hiss / Sizzling in our country's grassy language.' The commination which follows is, presumably, not directed only against medieval Pisa; and when it dilapidates to its conclusion in the pathos of naming the dead – 'Your atrocity was Theban. They were young / And innocent:

Hugh and Brigata / And the other two whose names are in my song' – we remember too the names of those other dead in the 'song' of *Field Work* itself. The art of the volume is to have held tensely in the same balance the song of possible reconciliation, and the memorial lament. All great art, Heaney has said, is in some sense comforting; but if *Field Work* is comforting, it is with a comfort earned well on the other side of human misery.

VI

Writing a Bare Wire:
Station Island (1984)

There are some lines in poetry which are like wool in
texture and some that are like bare wires. I was devoted to
a Keatsian woolly line, textured stuff, but now I would
like to be able to write a bare wire.

Seamus Heaney to Fintan O'Toole, 1984

Station Island, by far Seamus Heaney's longest book, is
in three separate parts: an opening section of individual
lyrics which take their occasions from the occurrences
and memories of the ordinary life; the central section,
the title sequence itself, which narrates, or dramatizes,
a number of encounters, in dream or in vision, with the
dead; and a concluding sequence, 'Sweeney Redivivus',
which is, as Heaney puts it in one of his notes to the
volume, 'voiced for Sweeney', the seventh-century king
transformed into a bird, whose story Heaney has trans-
lated from the medieval Irish poem *Buile Suibhne* as
Sweeney Astray.

Despite its separate parts, the book also has a formal
unity, however, signalled by the presence, in all three
parts, of the Sweeney figure. He is there in the poem
which ends Part One, 'The King of the Ditchbacks'
(which is, partly, about the act of translation itself);
then in the opening section of 'Station Island', in his
manifestation as the unregenerate Simon Sweeney, one
of a family of tinkers remembered from Heaney's child-
hood (the introduction to *Sweeney Astray* explicitly

[153]

links this Sweeney with the legendary character); and finally, of course, in the 'Sweeney Redivivus' sequence itself. What 'The King of the Ditchbacks' calls Sweeney's 'dark morse' is therefore tapped throughout the volume; and what the code spells out is an extraordinarily rigorous scrutiny by Seamus Heaney of his own commitments and attachments to his people, and of his responsibilities as a poet. This self-scrutiny proceeds through all three parts of *Station Island* in different modes. In Part One, it is pursued, sometimes implicitly, in separate lyrics originating in autobiographical experience; in 'Station Island', this contemporary self undergoes a penitential exercise in self-examination on a mythologized purgatorial pilgrimage; and in 'Sweeney Redivivus', the newly steadied self is released from its *Purgatorio* into the freedom of a kind of anti-self or parallel-self, as Heaney's voice is twinned with that of the character whose name rhymes with his own, 'Sweeney'.

The different voices of the volume – the lyric; the narrative and dramatic; the disguised or ventriloquial – are perhaps designed partly to offset the dangers of self-importance in this very self-involved book. They are, nevertheless, all chosen modalities of the voice of Seamus Heaney himself; and, in this sense, the shortest poem in *Station Island*, and one of its most perfect, 'Widgeon', may be read as an allegory of the book's procedure:

> It had been badly shot.
> While he was plucking it
> he found, he says, the voice box –
>
> like a flute stop
> in the broken windpipe –
>
> and blew upon it
> unexpectedly
> his own small widgeon cries.

[154]

This tiny anecdote about the shot wild duck is a story already told ('he says') – like the already much written-over pilgrimage to Station Island, like the *Buile Suibhne* – which Heaney now tells again, in his own words. The bird is 'badly shot', as some of the shades in 'Station Island' have been badly (wickedly, cruelly) shot, in Northern sectarian murders. 'He' in 'Widgeon' blows his own cries on the dead bird's voice box, just as Heaney briefly and poignantly returns a voice to the dead in the 'Station Island' sequence, a voice which remains, never-theless, entirely his own voice too; and as, in 'Sweeney Redivivus', his own voice sounds through the 'voice box' of Sweeney, the bird-man.

In this dartingly implicit allegory of the way the individual poetic voice speaks through the real and the legendary dead – through biographical experience and through literary tradition – it is the word 'unexpectedly', given a line to itself, which carries the greatest charge of implication: the poet who would properly – without sentimentality, without self-importance – articulate his own small widgeon cries through encounters with the dead must seem uncalculatingly preoccupied with his subject or with the form of his own poem, having something of the intent self-forgetfulness of one who would, testingly and probingly, attempt to blow upon a dead bird's voice box. The preoccupation may then release, 'unexpectedly', and almost distractedly, a genuine self-illumination or self-definition, just as 'Widgeon' releases allegorical implications most 'un-expectedly' too.

It is precisely this unexpectedness which makes the best work of *Station Island* so bracing. The scheme of the volume is an ambitious one, and, in my opinion, the book is not equally successful in all its parts. Neverthe-less, *Station Island* gives notice that Heaney's poetry, in its dissatisfied revision of earlier attitudes and

presumptions, and in its exploratory inventiveness as it
feels out new directions for itself, is now in the process
of successfully negotiating what is, for any poet, the
most difficult phase of a career – the transition from
the modes and manners which have created the repu-
tation, to the genuinely new and unexpected thing. It
is a poetry, in *Station Island*, bristling with the risks
and the dangers of such self-transformation but, at its
high points, triumphantly self-vindicating too.

I want to spend most of the space available to me in this
chapter discussing the two long sequences in *Station
Island*, since they present particular difficulties which
may be aided by sustained consideration. However, the
individual lyrics of Part One also represent something
new in Heaney's poetic voice: they have a harsher, more
astringent quality than the richly sensuous music of
Field Work. This is impelled by the preoccupations
which they share with the book's sequences, as Heaney's
rueful self-scrutiny is pursued in poems in which the
objects and occasions of the ordinary world (rather than,
as in 'Station Island', the visitations of ghosts) insist
their moral claims on the poet.

In 'An Aisling in the Burren' there are, literally,
sermons in stones – 'That day the clatter of stones / as
we climbed was a sermon / on conscience and healing';
and in poem after poem Heaney listens to similar, if
less explicit, sermons, as the natural world offers
instances of the exemplary. Sloe gin, in the marvellous
poem it gets to itself, is 'bitter / and dependable'; a
lobster is 'the hampered one, out of water, / fortified
and bewildered'; a granite chip from Joyce's Martello
tower is 'a Calvin edge in my complaisant pith'; old
pewter says that 'Glimmerings are what the soul's
composed of'; the Pacific in Malibu is an instruction in
how one is indissolubly wedded to the ascetic Atlantic;

visiting Hardy's birthplace is an education in displacement; flying a kite is to know 'the strumming, rooted, long-tailed pull of grief'; listening in to 'the limbo of lost words' on a loaning is to hear how

> At the click of a cell lock somewhere now
> the interrogator steels his *introibo*,
> the light-motes blaze, a blood-red cigarette
> startles the shades, screeching and beseeching.

These instructive moralities make Part One of *Station Island* severe and self-admonitory, and the astringent lyric voice, if it is willing to be counselled, is also chastened, restrained and wearied. As a result, a number of these poems sustain a sad note of diminishment and loss, a sense of transience and of the perilous fragmentariness of memory. 'What guarantees things keeping / if a railway can be lifted / like a long briar out of ditch growth?', Heaney asks in 'Iron Spike'; and the pathos attaching to what has disappeared is one of the essential marks of these poems: they are, I think, Heaney's first real exercises in nostalgia. If the newly tart lyric manner is a departure of the kind recommended in 'Making Strange' by the voice of poetry itself – 'Go beyond what's reliable / in all that keeps pleading and pleading' – the departure is nevertheless fully conscious of how much must be left behind: 'The Loaning' confesses that 'When you are tired or terrified / your voice slips back into its old first place / and makes the sound your shades make there . . .'

Despite the new departures of these lyrics, however, what nevertheless keeps pleading at some level in a number of them is the political reality of the North. In 'Sandstone Keepsake', another stone acts as the spur to a meditation in which Heaney paints a wry self-portrait of the artist as political outsider which is characteristic in its shrug of uneasy self-deprecation. The poem re-

members how the stone was 'lifted' from the beach at
Inishowen. At the northern tip of Co. Donegal,
Inishowen is at the opposite side of Lough Foyle from
the Magilligan internment camp. Heaney is therefore
prompted into mythologizing the stone in the terms of
a Dantean analogy, imagining it as 'A stone from
Phlegethon, / bloodied on the bed of hell's hot river';
but he rejects the grandiose comparison in deflating
embarrassment ('but not really'), before concluding the
poem in the self-deflating contemplation of how he
might appear to the Magilligan guards:

> Anyhow, there I was with the wet red stone
> in my hand, staring across at the watch-towers
> from my free state of image and allusion,
> swooped on, then dropped by trained binoculars:
>
> a silhouette not worth bothering about,
> out for the evening in scarf and waders
> and not about to set times wrong or right,
> stooping along, one of the venerators.

The incapacity for the political role is subtly rebuked
in those lines by the pun which makes over the 'Irish
Free State' into a phrase for the disengagement of
poetry, and by the allusion itself which refuses the
obligation Hamlet finds so overwhelming, to 'set right'
the times that are 'out of joint'. 'Sandstone Keepsake'
inherits, it may be, the guilt and anxiety of 'Exposure',
but seems more ironically assured of the poet's per-
ipheral status: the most the poem may aspire to is the
'veneration' of the political victim. This self-presen-
tation, with its let-downs and erosions, casts its
shadow far into *Station Island*.

'Station Island'

Station Island, or St Patrick's Purgatory, is a small,

rocky isle in the middle of Lough Derg in Co. Donegal which, since early medieval times, has been a place of pilgrimage for Irish Catholics. The three-day pilgrimage (which Seamus Heaney himself made three times in his youth) involves a self-punitive routine of prayer, fasting and barefoot walking around stone circles or 'beds', thought to be the remains of ancient monastic cells. From the very earliest times, Lough Derg has inspired popular legend and literature, in particular medieval accounts of miracles and visions, and historical narratives about the suppression of the pilgrimage in the eighteenth century, under the anti-Catholic Penal Laws. As a result, 'Station Island' is the name for a nexus of Irish Catholic religious, historical and cultural affiliations.

Since the nineteenth century, it has also been the subject of more specifically literary treatments: William Carleton's mocking but fascinated prose account, 'The Lough Derg Pilgrim' (1828); Patrick Kavanagh's lengthy *Lough Derg: A Poem* (written in 1942, but only published posthumously in 1978); Denis Devlin's characteristically portentous and frenzied poem, *Lough Derg* (1946); and Sean O'Faolain's well-known short story, 'The Lovers of the Lake' (1958), a story about the uneasy coexistence of sexuality and the Irish Catholic conscience. In a published talk touching on 'Station Island', 'Envies and Identifications: Dante and the Modern Poet', Heaney says that it was partly the anxiety occasioned by these numerous earlier literary versions of the pilgrimage which turned him to Dante's meetings with ghosts in the *Purgatorio* as a model for his own poem: Dante showed him how to 'make an advantage of what could otherwise be regarded as a disadvantage'. Inheriting from *Field Work*'s interest in Dante, Heaney therefore makes his imaginary pilgrimage to the island a series of meetings with ghosts of the type Dante meets in the *Purgatorio* – friendly, sad, self-defining, exemplary, admonitory, rebuking.

A central passage from 'Envies and Identifications' illuminates the relationship between Heaney and Dante in the sequence:

> What I first loved in the *Commedia* was the local intensity, the vehemence and fondness attaching to individual shades, the way personalities and values were emotionally soldered together, the strong strain of what has been called personal realism in the celebration of bonds of friendship and bonds of enmity. The way in which Dante could place himself in an historical world yet submit that world to scrutiny from a perspective beyond history, the way he could accommodate the political and the transcendent, this too encouraged my attempt at a sequence of poems which would explore the typical strains which the consciousness labours under in this country. The main tension is between two often contradictory commands: to be faithful to the collective historical experience and to be true to the recognitions of the emerging self. I hoped that I could dramatize these strains by meeting shades from my own dream-life who had also been inhabitants of the actual Irish world. They could perhaps voice the claims of orthodoxy and the necessity to recognize those claims. They could probe the validity of one's commitment.

The shades Heaney meets in the poem, then, have all been 'inhabitants of the actual Irish world', whether personally known friends and acquaintances, or writers known from their work; and their conversations turn, in some way, on the living of a proper life or on the production of a proper work. The revenants are advisers, from beyond the grave, on the poet's responsibilities in the realms of morality and of art.

In I, a prelude to the pilgrimage itself, the encounter, on a Sunday, is with the unregenerate 'sabbath-breaker', Simon Sweeney, a figure of fascination as well as fear, with his advice to 'Stay clear of all processions'. The advice is set against the orthodox pieties of a crowd of women on their way to mass, in a scene which contains (in 'the field was full / of half-remembered faces') a sudden echo of the opening of the medieval poem of vision and pilgrimage, *Piers Plowman*, and its 'field full of folk' – a reminder that poetry in English, as well as in Italian, has its tradition of the dream-vision, and that 'Station Island' self-consciously inherits from it. In II, the ghost is William Carleton, encountered appropriately on the road to Lough Derg, and not on the island itself, since, after visiting Station Island in his youth, he subsequently renounced Catholicism and wrote 'The Lough Derg Pilgrim' as a denunciation of its barbarities and superstitions (hence the reference to 'the old fork-tongued turncoat'). The 'ghost' of III is the inanimate 'seaside trinket' which, for Heaney as a child, had been redolent of the death of the girl who owned it (she was, in fact, Agnes, the sister of Heaney's father, who died of TB in the 1920s).

In Section IV Heaney meets a priest who had died on the foreign missions shortly after his ordination. (This was a man called Terry Keenan, still a clerical student when Heaney knew him.) The section meditates on the ratifying role of the priesthood in Irish society, and its effect on the priest himself, 'doomed to the decent thing'. V includes three separate encounters with teachers or mentors of Heaney's, including his first teacher at Anahorish School, Barney Murphy, and – interestingly in this context – Patrick Kavanagh. VI recalls, with affectionate tenderness, a very early sexual experience and, after 'long virgin / Fasts and thirsts' under the dominion of Catholic doctrine on sexual morality, a later satisfying and fulfilling one. The ghost of VII is a man Heaney had played football with in his youth, the victim of a sectarian murder in

Northern Ireland. (Heaney is remembering William Strathearn, killed by two off-duty policemen in a particularly notorious incident in Co. Antrim.) The victim's description of the circumstances of his death impels Heaney into a confession of what he regards as his own evasive, uncommitted politics. VIII confronts Heaney with two further ghosts whose challenges provoke self-rebuke – Tom Delaney, an archaeologist friend who died tragically young at thirty-two, towards whom Heaney feels 'I had somehow broken / covenants, and failed an obligation', and Colum McCartney, the subject of 'The Strand at Lough Beg' in *Field Work*, who utters the most unrelenting accusation in the sequence, '"for the way you whitewashed ugliness and drew / the lovely blinds of the *Purgatorio* / and saccharined my death with morning dew"'.

Section IX gives a voice to one of the ten IRA hunger-strikers who died in Long Kesh between March and September 1981. (Heaney is actually thinking of the second of them to die, Francis Hughes, who came from his own district, Bellaghy, and whose family he knows.) The certitude which could lead to that kind of political suicide is juxtaposed with a dream of release and revival in which the extraordinary symbol of a 'strange polyp' ('My softly awash and blanching self-disgust') appears, to be supported and illuminated by a candle, and is followed by a further symbol of possibility, an 'old brass trumpet' remembered from childhood. X has another inanimate ghost, a drinking mug removed from Heaney's childhood home by actors for use in a play, and returned as Ronan's psalter is miraculously returned from the lake by an otter at the opening of *Sweeney Astray* – a further symbol for the unexpected translations the known, ordinary and domestic may undergo.

In XI the ghost is a monk to whom Heaney once

made his confession and who, suggesting that Heaney should 'Read poems as prayers', asked him to translate something by St John of the Cross, the sixteenth-century Spanish mystic, as a penance. Heaney responds now, belatedly, with his version of 'Cantar del alma que se huelga de conoscer a Dios por fe', the 'Song of the soul that is glad to know God by faith', a hymn to the 'fountain' of the Trinity to be discovered within the sacrament of the Eucharist, that sign of the believing Church in harmonious community. Finally, in the concluding section of the poem, Heaney, back on the mainland, meets the ghost of James Joyce, who recommends a course antithetical to that of orthodox Catholic pilgrimage, a striking-out on one's own in an isolation which, Joyce claims, is the only way the poet's proper work can be done.

These individual encounters find their basic structural shape in the nature of the pilgrimage itself – leaving the ordinary social world, crossing the waters of Lough Derg, and then returning to that world with some kind of refreshment and new clarity. The irony of 'Station Island', however, is that this pilgrimage leads to no confirmation in the religion and values of the tribe, but to something very like a renunciation of them. It is possible to read the sequence as a kind of reverse palinode, directed at some of the innate assumptions and attitudes of Heaney's own earlier work – a palinode which actually rejects the orthodox communal doctrine and morality, rather than giving final assent to them. When Heaney does 'repent' in IX, it is the old tribal complicities which are imagined as immature and self-restricting: '"I repent / My unweaned life that kept me competent / To sleepwalk with connivance and mistrust."' Heaney is tentative about his repentance, ironically aware of all the ways in which one must remain permanently 'unweaned' from such powerful formative influences and experiences, and the poem has, throughout, the poignancy of anxiety and misgiving. Nevertheless, 'Station Island' uses the metaphor of its Irish Catholic pilgrimage to define some of the constrictions which that religion and culture have imposed on one individual consciousness, and to suggest how, under alternative mentors, and through art, a newly enabling freedom might be gained.

It is possible to read out of the earlier parts of the poem a subtext of accusations against Catholicism: in I, where Heaney is set, behind the pious women, on a 'drugged path', that it acts as a mere opiate, numbing the obedient conscience with its claims of authority; in II, where the radical Ribbonmen of Carleton's day have become, by the time of Heaney's childhood, a drunken band who 'played hymns to Mary', that it keeps you patient and enduring, incapable of the anger of action; in III, where the child's death, held in pious memory, is juxtaposed with the brute animal reality of a dog's death, that, in attempting to account for death, it in fact refuses to face its reality, and sentimentalizes it; and in IV, with its 'doomed' priest, that Irish clericalism thwarts the lives of those who represent it, and bolsters the platitudinous pieties of those it 'serves'. In the latter sections of the poem, Catholicism is heavily implicated in Heaney's adolescence of sexual dissatisfaction and guilt, and in his unease and regret about his lack of any firmer political commitment – the 'timid circumspect involvement' for which he begs forgiveness of Strathearn, and that confusion of 'evasion and artistic tact' of which McCartney accuses him. All of these charges generate the outburst of rejection in section IX – "'I hate how quick I was to know my place. / I hate where I was born, hate everything / That made me biddable and unforthcoming"' – where knowing his place is both establishing an identity with a particular territory (celebrated as a virtue often enough in the earlier work) and also meekly accepting a servitude to the mores of a community (where to 'know your place' is to stay put).

Even though it quickly undercuts itself with rueful qualifications, the venom of that climactic attack makes it unsurprising that, despite appearances, no true pilgrimage is actually undertaken in the poem. In IV, Heaney is 'ready to say the dream words *I renounce* . . .', the renunciation of worldliness which is the essential prelude to repentance, when he is interrupted by the priest wondering if Heaney is on Station Island only to take the 'last look', and suggesting that, for him, the pilgrimage is without its essential point – 'the god has, as they say, withdrawn'. No orthodox praying is done on the pilgrimage: when he kneels in III, it is only 'Habit's afterlife'; and the poem-prayer in XI could be thought to undermine its song of faith with its constant refrain, 'although it is the night'. In John of the Cross this is the 'dark night of the soul', in which the mystic feels himself temporarily abandoned by God; but, to a more secular consciousness, it could equally well be the sheer inability to believe.

Heaney is also sometimes in physical positions which dissociate him from the other pilgrims: in V, he is 'faced wrong way / into more pilgrims absorbed in this exercise', and in VI, the others 'Trailed up the steps as I went down them / Towards the bottle-green, still / Shade of an oak'. That same section goes so far as to appropriate, from the beginning of the *Divine Comedy*, the moment when Dante is impelled on his journey by learning from Virgil of Beatrice's intercession, in order to describe Heaney's own sexual awakening after the enforced virginity of his Irish Catholic adolescence. The truant which Heaney is playing from the pilgrimage there turns the tradition of the vision-poem on its head, making sexual not divine love the object of the exercise; but it reminds us too that Dante's great poem of Christian quest discovers its images of heavenly bliss in a transfigured human woman.

At the centre of Heaney's pilgrimage, however, there is not presence but absence, figured frequently as a 'space'. It is 'a space utterly empty, / utterly a source, like the idea of sound' in III; 'A stillness far away, a space' in VI; 'the granite airy space / I was staring into' in VIII; and, in XII, after the pilgrimage, 'It was as if I had stepped free into a space / alone with nothing that I had not known / already'. This final linking of the blank space with freedom comes after Heaney has been counselled by Joyce; and the whole of 'Station Island' discovers its enabling and releasing alternative in its exemplary artist figures. Joyce is, implicitly, the repository of a new kind of personal and cultural health when Heaney takes his hand 'like a convalescent' and feels an 'alien comfort' in his company. In this sense, the pilgrimage to the island in the poem is a large parenthesis, the brackets of which are closed by William Carleton at one end, and by James Joyce at the other – artists offering, on the mainland, their alternatives to the orthodoxies of the island, alternatives which ironically echo the very first advice Heaney is given in the poem, the unregenerate Simon Sweeney's 'Stay clear of all processions'.

Carleton's essential significance for the poem is clarified by Heaney's essay, 'A tale of two islands', where 'The Lough Derg Pilgrim', with its portrait of a culturally and materially deprived Ireland, is opposed to Synge's much better known account, in his plays and prose, of the Aran Islands – in Heaney's opinion, a glamorizing of the reality in the interests of the Irish Literary

Revival. The 'two islands', 'Station' and 'Aran', represent two different Irelands, realities put to virtually opposed literary and ideological uses. Carleton, in fact, is regarded very much as a nineteenth-century equivalent of Patrick Kavanagh – a teller of the true tale, from the inside, but also from a position of estrangement, of Irish rural life ('not ennobling but disabling'). In his appearance in 'Station Island', he counsels Heaney in a righteous anger (of which Heaney knows himself – it seems, shamefully – incapable) and also in the redemptive necessity, for the Irish writer, of a memory and sensibility schooled by politics as well as by the natural world: '"We are earthworms of the earth, and all that / has gone through us is what will be our trace"'. The word associated with Carleton in 'Station Island' is 'hard'. Defining his 'turncoat' politics, Heaney has him say, '"If times were hard, I could be hard too"'; and when he departs in the final line, he 'headed up the road at the same hard pace'.

His hardness is matched by Joyce's 'straightness'. In XII, 'he walked straight as a rush / upon his ash plant, his eyes fixed straight ahead'; and when he departs, 'the downpour loosed its screens round his straight walk'. This is the straightness of his decisiveness and authority, as he counsels the more pliable Heaney in a course opposed to tribal and local fidelities. This account of Joyce spells out more clearly some of the implications of Leopold Bloom's appearance at the end of 'Traditions' in *Wintering Out*. What Heaney jokingly calls the 'Feast of the Holy Tundish' is a very secular feast, constructed from Stephen's diary entry for 13 April, at the end of *A Portrait of the Artist*. The entry is 'a revelation / / set among my stars' because 13 April is Heaney's birthday. In the passage referred to, Stephen is remembering an earlier conversation with an English Jesuit about the word 'tundish'. The priest has never heard the word before, but it is a common usage for 'funnel' in Stephen's Dublin:

> That tundish has been on my mind for a long time. I looked it up and find it English and good old blunt English too. Damn the dean of studies and his funnel! What did he come here for to teach us his own language or to learn it from us? Damn him one way or the other!

The damnation of the Englishman is a register of Joyce's supreme confidence in his own language, and this is a releasing and enabling moment, a 'password', for Heaney, who inherits in his own art the necessity of conveying uniquely Irish experience in the English language as it is spoken in Ireland. Hence Heaney's addressing Joyce as 'old father', as Stephen addresses the mythical Daedalus at the end of the *Portrait* (and as Heaney had already addressed the Vikings in *North*).

The confidence is combined, in Joyce, with that arrogant pride and disdain which enabled him, as Heaney has put it in *Among Schoolchildren*, to 'deconstruct the prescriptive myths of Irishness'. Hence Joyce's concluding advice to Heaney, in this poetic undertaking which may be said similarly to deconstruct such myths, to 'keep at a tangent', to

> 'swim

> out on your own and fill the element
> with signatures on your own frequency,
> echo soundings, searches, probes, allurements,

> elver-gleams in the dark of the whole sea.'

Given the interest and complexity of its conception, and the personal urgency of its themes, it is unfortunate that, in my opinion, 'Station Island' is far from entirely successful. There are some excellent things in it. Section III, for instance, with its extraordinarily inward and intimate evocation of the way the young

Heaney is almost erotically possessed by the child's death, is as good as anything he has written. And the poem's most Dantean moments – McCartney's rebuke, and the fading of some of the shades – have the kind of heartbreaking poignancy which shows the lessons learnt from the 'Ugolino' translation in *Field Work*.

Nevertheless, it seems to me that the narrative and dramatic structure of the sequence is peculiarly inhibiting to Heaney's truest poetic gifts and touch. The encounters come to seem predictable and over-schematic. The dialogue is sometimes very heavy handed: 'Open up and see what you have got' and 'Not that it is any consolation, / but they were caught' are jaw-breakingly unlikely from people in any kind of passion. The symbols seem over-insistent, particularly when one remembers the great grace and delicacy with which the literal slips into the symbolic in some of the earlier work. There are moments of distinct bathos: when, in IX, after seeing the vision of the trumpet, Heaney tells us he 'pitched backwards in a headlong fall', and we are suddenly closer to slapstick than to symbolic reverie; and, more subtly perhaps, when the Joycean voice of XII seems so much more accommodating, concerned and hortatory than anything Joyce ever wrote himself – for the good reason, perhaps, that its marine imagery is much more Heaney-like than Joycean, much closer to 'Casualty' and 'Oysters' than to the *Portrait*. Finally, there are some uncertainties in the handling of verse form, particularly in Heaney's rather ragged variations on the Dantean *terza rima*. The form is notoriously difficult in English, but Heaney's variations on it are bound to summon much too closely for comfort Eliot's tremendous imitative approximation of it in the second section of 'Little Gidding', and Yeats's use of it in a poem Heaney admires in *Preoccupations*, 'Cuchulain Comforted'.

[169]

All of this is perhaps to say, in another way, that Seamus Heaney's true distinction as a poet is a lyric distinction, and that the successful larger forms he has so far found are forms which accommodate, even while they provoke and extend, his lyricism. While I cannot think that 'Station Island' with its narrative and dramatic exigencies, is such a form, it is clearly a necessary poem for Heaney to have written, one that defines a painful realignment between himself and his own culture, and brings him to that point of newly steadied illumination where it might be said of his work, as it is said of its symbol, the polyp supported by a candle, that 'the whole bright-masted thing retrieved / A course and the currents it had gone with / Were what it rode and showed.'

'Sweeney Redivivus'

Seamus Heaney's engagement with the figure of Sweeney from the medieval Irish poem *Buile Suibhne* lasted over ten years – from his earliest attempts at a translation in 1972 until its eventual publication, as *Sweeney Astray*, in 1983 in Ireland and in 1984 in England. Sweeney, in the poem, is a possibly real seventh-century Ulster king who offends the cleric St Ronan, and is punished by being cursed after the Battle of Moira in 637. Driven mad and transformed into a bird, he flies, exiled from family and tribe, over Ireland and as far as Scotland. The poem's narrative is frequently interrupted by Sweeney's poignant lyric expressions of his own misery, and by his equally sharp and tender celebrations of the Irish landscape, particularly its trees. Sweeney is therefore, as well as being a mad, exiled king, a lyric poet; and in Robert Graves's account of *Buile Suibhne* in *The White Goddess* he describes it as 'the most ruthless and bitter description in all European literature of an obsessed poet's predicament'.

Heaney recognizes in the poem a crucial point in the changeover from a pagan to a Christian culture in Ireland, and he is also interested in it for political and topographical reasons; but in the introduction to his version, he spells out too some of the implications of a recognition similar to Graves's:

> ... insofar as Sweeney is also a figure of the artist, displaced, guilty, assuaging himself by his utterance, it is possible to read the work as an aspect of the quarrel between free creative imagination and the constraints of religious, political and domestic obligation.

A further aspect, in fact, of that 'quarrel' already evident in 'Station Island'; and it is difficult to read far into Heaney's version of *Buile Suibhne* without sensing some of the ways in which Sweeney's voice is harmonized with, or subdued to, Heaney's own. Sweeney uses a vocabulary familiar from Heaney's own poems – 'visitant', 'casualties', 'recitation', 'trust', 'philander', 'teems of rain', 'A sup of water. Watercress', as well as employing the thin quatrain as his most frequent lyric form. At one point, indeed, the original is 'translated' in lines which are wryly self-referential: at the conclusion of section 67, Sweeney says:

> I have deserved all this:
> night-vigils, terror,
> flittings across water,
> women's cried-out eyes.

This is another version of a sentence which concludes 'The wanderer', one of the prose-poems in *Stations*, which mythologizes Heaney's departure from his first school – 'That day I was a rich young man, who could tell you now of flittings, night-vigils, let-downs, women's cried-out eyes'.

That 'rich young man' reappears in the final poem of the 'Sweeney Redivivus' sequence, 'On the Road'. In the gospel narrative of Matthew XIX, the man asks Christ what he must do to be saved, and the answer is the uncompromisingly absolute one which Heaney repeats in his poem, 'Sell all you have and give to the poor and follow me.' The demand, whether it is made in the realm of religion or of art, and whether a response to it is a real possibility or a chimera, is one that haunts the sequence, and in a sense encloses it, since 'The King of the Ditchbacks' in Part One ends in lines which bind Heaney, Sweeney and the rich young man together. That poem has brilliantly evoked the mesmerized and obsessive process of poetic translation ('He was depending on me as I hung out on the limb of a translated phrase. . . . Small dreamself in the branches') before its final section effects this further 'translation' which carries Heaney over, in an imagined magical rite, into Sweeney:

> And I saw myself
> rising to move in that dissimulation,
>
> top-knotted, masked in sheaves, noting
> the fall of birds: a rich young man
>
> leaving everything he had
> for a migrant solitude.

Heaney translates himself into Sweeney, then, in the context of a biblical allusion which summons to the metamorphosis notions of urgent demand, of striking out on one's own, of exile, of attempting to go beyond what is recognized and known. They make it clear why Heaney told Seamus Deane in 1977 that he thought he had discovered in Sweeney 'a presence, a fable which could lead to the discovery of feelings in myself which I could not otherwise find words for, and which would cast a dream or possibility or myth across the swirl of private feelings: an objective correlative'.

It is clear that this 'migrant solitude' is akin to the 'tangent' recommended by Joyce at the end of 'Station Island', and the actual form of the poems of 'Sweeney Redivivus' seems to bear some relation to Heaney's description of Joyce's voice, 'definite / as a steel nib's downstroke' (in *Ulysses*, Stephen refers to 'the cold steelpen' of his art). There is a definiteness, a hard edge, a sense of the thing suddenly and speedily, but finally, articulated in Heaney's free forms in these poems. They have something of the quick cut and sharpness of a trial piece, compared to what seems to me the worked over and occasionally congealed finish of 'Station Island'. In this, their forms clearly also inherit from Heaney's view of medieval Irish lyric, as he expresses it in 'The God in the Tree' in *Preoccupations*. In that essay, he compliments Flann O'Brien (who had made his own use of Sweeney in his novel, *At Swim-Two-Birds*) for his characterization of the 'steel-pen exactness' of Irish lyric; and he also describes such lyric himself in terms appropriate to his own sequence – its 'little jabs of delight in the elemental', its combination of 'suddenness and richness', and its revelation of the writer as 'hermit' as much as 'scribe' ('Sweeney Redivivus' includes poems called 'The Hermit' and 'The Scribes').

I think it is worth adducing this larger context for 'Sweeney Redivivus', a context in which a hard and sharp kind of Irish literature puts its pressure on Heaney, since the Sweeney of *Buile Suibhne* is really only one chord of Heaney's voice in the sequence; and, despite the description, in a note, of the poems as 'glosses' on the original story, there are in fact remarkably few obvious points of correspondence. 'Sweeney' in 'Sweeney Redivivus' is the name for a personality, a

[173]

different self, a congruence of impulses, a mask anti-
thetical to much that the name 'Seamus Heaney' has
meant in his previous books. In 'Envies and Identifi-
cations', Heaney defines the Yeatsian mask in terms
which seem relevant to 'Sweeney':

> Energy is discharged, reality is revealed and enforced
> when the artist strains to attain the mask of his opposite;
> in the act of summoning and achieving that image, he
> does his proper work and leaves us with the art itself,
> which is a kind of trace element of the inner struggle of
> opposites, a graph of the effort of transcendence.

Yeats himself is, I presume, 'The Master' in the poem
of that title in the sequence, which could be written
almost as an allegory of what the critic Harold Bloom
has called the 'anxiety of influence': the 'master' as the
precursor, the poet against whom Heaney's own art
must struggle in order properly to define and articulate
itself. Heaney imagines Yeats as a 'rook' in the 'tower'
of, presumably, his art and of his Protestant Ascendancy
culture (just as Yeats did live in a tower, and entitled
one of his major books *The Tower*); and the gradual
coming to terms with him is the discovery that 'his
book of withholding / . . . was nothing / arcane, just the
old rules / we all had inscribed on our slates', the
discovery that Yeats's notoriously private mythology
conceals an apprehensible human and political mean-
ing and relevance. Heaney's measuring of himself
against this magisterial authority, which has sounded
the Sweeney note of enterprising, wily self-assertion, is
also, however, combined with an envious humility –

> How flimsy I felt climbing down
> the unrailed stairs on the wall,
> hearing the purpose and venture
> in a wingflap above me.

– and the poem is the trace not so much of a struggle, as

of a bold but wary inspection, a revelation of how to be unafraid which is the measure of one's own authority.

That this poem is an allegory is typical of the sequence, in which allegory and parable, the puzzling and the hermetic, are the constant modes. In fact, one of Heaney's major derivations from the original source is – as the master-as-rook suggests – a series of ornithological correspondences. 'The First Flight', for instance, views Heaney's move from Belfast to Glanmore as a bird's migration; 'Drifting Off', a version of a medieval 'Boast' poem, ascribes different human (or poetic) qualities to birds; 'A Waking Dream' imagines poetic composition as the attempt to catch a bird by throwing salt on its tail (as the popular recommendation has it), but in fact being transported into flight oneself; and 'On the Road' actually locates the moment when Heaney, previously behind the wheel of a car, is lofted into flight ('I was up and away'). Apart from this system of analogy, what the original story offers 'Sweeney Redivivus' is little more than a medieval-anchorite colouring in some poems, and a tolerant hospitality to others which could just as easily have appeared without its support-system – 'In the Beech', for instance, which imagines the young Heaney in a tree, and the brilliant 'Holly'. Indeed, three poems which appear towards the end of the sequence – 'An Artist' (on Cézanne), 'The Old Icons' (on republican politics) and 'In Illo Tempore' (on the loss of religious faith) seem written more straightforwardly in Heaney's own voice, though by now clearly schooled into a 'Sweeney' scepticism and distrust.

Although the mask, then, is not worn consistently in the sequence, 'The Master' suggests its usefulness to Heaney. There it allows him the opportunity to articulate in a parable what would otherwise be virtually impossible without pretension or overweening vanity, the measuring of himself against Yeats. Elsewhere, it allows him a similar pride in his own achievement, and a tangential, dubious, sideways-on inspection of some matters already handled more straightforwardly in his earlier work. This is why 'The First Gloss' steps from its 'justified line / into the margin' only after recalling, in the metaphor, 'the shaft of the pen', the first poem in Heaney's first collection, 'Digging'. And it is why, in the poem, 'Sweeney Redivivus', and in 'Unwinding', Heaney pursues the metaphor of his head as 'a ball of wet twine / dense with soakage, but beginning / to unwind'. The 'twine' – the string made by joining together, 'twinning', two separate strands – is both Heaney and Sweeney. Its 'unwinding' is Heaney's studied attempt to dry out the 'soakage' of his heritage and, perhaps, of his more acceptable, pliable social self.

The sequence as a whole may be thought to define different stages in this process of unwinding as, in a newly suspicious perspective, Heaney reviews his life and reputation. 'In the Beech' and 'The First Kingdom' suggest how selective his earliest accounts of his first world were. 'In The Beech' sets the young Heaney in a 'boundary tree' between the old rural ways and modern military industrialism (he is thinking, I presume, of the British airforce bases in Northern Ireland during the Second World War): the latter, of course, made no appearance in *Death of a Naturalist*. 'The First Kingdom' takes a more jaundiced view of the inhabitants of that world than one would have believed possible from the author of Heaney's first book: 'And seed, breed and generation still / they are holding on, every bit / as pious and exacting and demeaned' – where 'exacting' perhaps looks back rebukingly to the 'exact' revenge of 'Punishment'.

Similarly, 'The First Flight', 'Drifting Off' and 'The

Scribes' imply a more unapologetic confidence in his own work than is apparent in anything Heaney has previously written. 'The First Flight' celebrates, with a Joycean disdain, his outwitting of adverse criticism ('they began to pronounce me / a feeder off battlefields' leaps out of the parable into contemporary literary battlefields for anyone who remembers some Northern accounts of *North*); 'Drifting Off' ends with Heaney not as the Joycean 'hawklike man', but as the hawk himself, 'unwieldy / and brimming, / my spurs at the ready'; and 'The Scribes' is an almost contemptuous jousting with, again, his critics (or his peers?), which culminates when Heaney/Sweeney throws this poem itself in their faces: 'Let them remember this not inconsiderable / contribution to their jealous art.' That 'not inconsiderable' is finely judged, keeping its temper along with its *hauteur*, utterly certain that it is 'considerable'; and the poem has something of that insolence Heaney once admired in Nadezhda Mandelstam's treatment of the Soviets, 'the unthinking authority of somebody brushing a fly from her food'. This is the reverse of accommodating, it is dangerous, and one would not like to get on the wrong side of it; but its tone allies Heaney with an Irish tradition to which he has not previously given great allegiance, one that includes eighteenth-century Gaelic poetry and Austin Clarke, for instance, as well as Joyce. Heaney has chosen – temporarily, perhaps – to call this tradition 'Sweeney'; but, under whatever name, it is a salutary guard against certain kinds of sweetness and lushness which have whispered at the edge of earshot in some of his styles.

These asperities of tone are softened by a certain regretfulness in those poems in the sequence which once again review Heaney's attitude to religion and to politics. 'The Cleric', on Catholicism, seems to acknowledge, ruefully, at its close that, having once placed faith in all of that, any future sense of freedom from it will be defined by it – the familiar enough double-bind of the devout lapsed Catholic, but phrased here, in the tones of the still-pagan Sweeney reflecting on St Ronan, in a way which gives genuinely new life to the old song:

> Give him his due, in the end

> he opened my path to a kingdom
> of such scope and neuter allegiance
> my emptiness reigns at its whim.

'In Illo Tempore' – its title taken from the words which introduced the reading of the gospel in the old Latin mass – is perhaps Heaney's most straightforward and personal rehearsal of the theme (released, it may be, by the Sweeney mask, but not much indebted to it). Imagining Catholicism as a language one has lost the ability to speak, consigning it to '*illo tempore*', 'that time', the poem is sadly resigned rather than gratefully released; and in this it is at one, perhaps, with the reverence still felt, at some level, for the outgrown republican images in 'The Old Icons' – 'Why, when it was all over, did I hold on to them?' In these poems, which are among the best in 'Sweeney Redivivus', resolve and regret merge to create a peculiarly chastened tone, which is also peculiarly honest.

The poem which closes 'Sweeney Redivivus', and the whole of *Station Island*, 'On the Road', may be read as a kind of summary of Heaney's career to date, and the statement of an intention for the future, as it inherits and brings to fulfilment the volume's imagery of journeying, pilgrimage, quest and migration. The poem opens with that figure common in the earlier work, Heaney-as-driver, but now with the driver behind the steering wheel's 'empty round'. This is an emptiness, a space suddenly filled with the rich young man's question about salvation. Christ's invitation, accompanied by the sudden 'visitation' of the last bird in *Station Island*, provokes a response in which Heaney is translated out of that early figure and its present emptiness, into Heaney-as-Sweeney. The flight which follows, with its swooping and dipping rhythms, seems similarly to translate Christ's injunction out of the realm of religion – Heaney/Sweeney migrating from 'chapel gable' and 'churchyard wall' – into the realm of art, as it ends inside a 'high cave mouth' beside the prehistoric cave drawing of a 'drinking deer'. This is presumably related to that 'deer of poetry . . . / in pools of lucent sound' which appears in 'A Migration' in Part One; but in 'On the Road', its nostril is 'flared / / at a dried-up source'. It is a source, nevertheless, which provides Heaney with at least the possibility of some arid renewal:

> For my book of changes
> I would meditate
> that stone-faced vigil
>
> until the long dumbfounded
> spirit broke cover
> to raise a dust
> in the font of exhaustion.

The 'font' in a church usually contains holy water, used to make the sign of the cross; but this dry 'font of exhaustion' is perhaps Seamus Heaney's equivalent of Yeats's 'foul rag-and-bone shop of the heart' at the end of 'The Circus Animals' Desertion', that point of desolation from which, alone, the new inspiration may rise. In that poem, Yeats reviews the stages of his career in some detail, and in 'On the Road', Heaney may be thought to review his own, more glancingly, in little verbal echoes of his earlier work. The road 'reeling in' remembers the roads that 'unreeled, unreeled' in that other poem of flight, 'Westering', at the end of *Wintering Out*; 'soft-nubbed' and 'incised outline' recall the archaeological diction of *North*, as the poem's chain of optatives ('I would roost . . .', 'I would migrate . . .', 'I would meditate . . .') make again one of the characteristic grammatical figures of *North*; the 'undulant, tenor/black-letter latin' recalls the 'sweet tenor latin' of 'Leavings', and the phrase 'broke cover' recalls the badger that 'broke cover in me' in 'The Badgers', both in *Field Work*. This unobtrusive self-allusiveness makes it plain how much in Heaney's earlier 'source' is now 'dried-up', and how much directed energy and effort must go into the construction of any new 'book of changes'.

This is the final stage of self-knowledge and self-declaration to which the Sweeney mask has brought Heaney; and I find the sequence of exceptional originality and authority. Sweeney has been a more subtle, responsive and intimate means of self-dramatization than the sometimes creaking machinery and over-earnestness of 'Station Island'. The mask has provided the opportunity for a new kind of autobiographical poetry – not 'confessionally' flat and presumptuous, not as edgily invisible as the Eliotic *personae*, not risking the sometimes histrionic grandiloquence of Yeats. Sweeney is, above all, the name for a restless dissatisfaction with the work already done, a fear of repetition, an anxiety about too casual an assimilation and acclaim, a deep suspicion of one's own reputation and excellence. He is, therefore, also an instruction to the critic, ending his account of a poet still in mid-career, against too definitive a conclusion. As Sweeney's creator and *alter ego* reminded John Haffenden, 'the tune isn't called for the poet, he calls the tune'.

Select bibliography

By Seamus Heaney

Books

Death of a Naturalist, London, 1966
Door into the Dark, London, 1969
Wintering Out, London, 1972
North, London, 1975
Field Work, London, 1979
Preoccupations: Selected Prose 1968–1978, London, 1980
Selected Poems 1965–1975, London, 1980
The Rattle Bag: An Anthology of Poetry, selected by Seamus
    Heaney and Ted Hughes, London, 1982
Sweeney Astray, Derry, 1983
Station Island, London, 1984
Sweeney Astray, London, 1984

A selection of limited editions and pamphlets

Eleven Poems, Belfast, 1965
A Lough Neagh Sequence, Manchester, 1969
Stations, Belfast, 1975
Bog Poems, London, 1975
Hedge School: Sonnets from Glanmore, Salem, Oregon, 1979
Ugolino, Dublin, 1979
Gravities: A Collection of Poems and Drawings, with Noel
    Connor, Newcastle upon Tyne, 1979
Poems and a Memoir, New York, 1982
An Open Letter, Derry, 1983
*Among Schoolchildren: A lecture dedicated to the memory of
    John Malone*, Belfast, 1983
Hailstones, Dublin, 1984

From the Republic of Conscience, Dublin, 1985
Place and Displacement: Recent Poetry of Northern Ireland,
 Grasmere, 1985

Uncollected articles and reviews, etc.

'A Chester Pageant', *The Use of English*, 17:1, Autumn 1965,
 pp. 58–60
'Out of London: Ulster's Troubles', *New Statesman*, 1 July
 1966, pp. 23–4
'Irish Eyes', *Listener*, 28 December 1967, pp. 851–3
'Old Derry's Walls', *Listener*, 24 October 1968, pp. 521–3
'Celtic Fringe, Viking Fringe', *Listener*, 21 August 1969,
 pp. 254–5
'King of the Dark', *Listener*, 5 February 1970, pp. 181–2
'King Conchobor and his Knights' (on Kinsella's version of
 the *Tain*), *Listener*, 26 March 1970, pp. 416–17
'Views' (from Berkeley), *Listener*, 31 December 1970, p. 903
Munro (transcript of a radio play), *Everyman*, no.3, 1970,
 pp. 58–65
'A Poet's Childhood', *Listener*, 1 November 1971, pp. 660–1
'After the Synge-song' (on Patrick Kavanagh), *Listener*,
 13 January 1972, pp. 55–6
'The Labourer and the Lord' (on Francis Ledwidge), *Listener*,
 28 September 1972, pp. 408–9
'Deep as England' (on Ted Hughes), *Hibernia*, 1 December
 1972, p. 13
'Mother Ireland', *Listener*, 7 December 1972, p. 790
Introduction to *Soundings*, Belfast, 1972
'Lost Ulstermen' (on John Montague's *The Rough Field*),
 Listener, 26 April 1973, pp. 550–1
'Poets on Poetry: Seamus Heaney', *Listener*, 8 November
 1973, p. 629
'Now and in England' (on David Jones's *The Sleeping Lord*),
 Spectator, 4 May 1974, p. 547
'Summoning Lazarus' (on P. V. Glob's *The Mound People*),
 Listener, 6 June 1974, pp. 741–2
'Shorts for Auden' (on Auden's *Collected Poems*), *Hibernia*,
 8 October 1976, p. 21

'The Poetry of Richard Murphy', *Irish University Review*,
Spring 1977, pp. 18–30

'John Bull's Other Island', *Listener*, 29 September 1977,
pp. 397–9

'The Interesting Case of John Alphonsus Mulrennan', *Planet*,
January 1978, pp. 34–40

'The Poet as a Christian', *The Furrow*, 29:10, October 1978,
pp. 603–6

'Kavanagh of the parish', *Listener*, 26 April 1979, pp. 577–8

'The Language of Exile' (on Derek Walcott), *Parnassus:
Poetry in Review*, Fall/Winter 1979, pp. 5–11

'Two Voices' (on A. D. Hope), *London Review of Books*,
20 March 1980, p. 8

'Treely and Rurally' (on Dante), *Quarto*, August 1980, p. 14

'. . . English and Irish' (on Brian Friel's *Translations*), *Times
Literary Supplement*, 24 October 1980, p. 1199

'Robert Lowell' (memorial address given at St Luke's Church,
London, on 5 October 1977), *Agenda*, 18:3, Autumn 1980,
pp. 23–8. This was also privately published by Faber in
1978.

'A tale of two islands: reflections on the Irish Literary
Revival', in P. J. Drudy (ed.), *Irish Studies 1*, Cambridge,
1980, pp. 1–20

'Current Unstated Assumptions about Poetry: 1', *Critical
Inquiry*, Summer 1981, pp. 645–51

'Osip and Nadezhda Mandelstam', *London Review of Books*,
20 August–2 September 1981, pp. 3–6

'The Main of Light' (on Philip Larkin), in Anthony Thwaite
(ed.), *Larkin at Sixty*, London, 1982, pp. 131–8

'The Fully Exposed Poem' (on Miroslav Holub), *Parnassus:
Poetry in Review*, Spring–Summer 1983, pp. 4–16

Preface to *The Crane Bag Book of Irish Studies*, ed.
M. P. Hederman and Richard Kearney, Gerrard's Cross,
1983

'A New and Surprising Yeats', *New York Times Book Review*,
18 March 1984, pp. 1, 35–6

'Making It New' (on James Fenton), *New York Review of
Books*, 25 October 1984, pp. 40–2

'Envies and Identifications: Dante and the Modern Poet',
  Irish University Review, 15:1, Spring 1985, pp. 5–19
'The Sensual Philosopher' (on Italo Calvino), *New York
  Times Book Review*, 29 September 1985, pp. 1, 60
Poetry Book Society Bulletin, 61 (Summer 1969); 85
  (Summer 1975); 102 (Autumn 1979); 123 (Winter 1984)

Interviews and profiles

'Le clivage traditionnel', *Les Lettres Nouvelles*, March 1973,
  pp. 187–9
Interview, with Harriet Cooke, *Irish Times*, 28 December
  1973, p. 8
'The Irish quest', with Raymond Gardner, *Guardian*,
  2 November 1974, p. 8
Interview, with Caroline Walsh, *Irish Times*, 6 December
  1975, p. 5
'Unhappy and at Home', with Seamus Deane, *The Crane Bag*,
  1:1, 1977, pp. 61–7. Reprinted in *The Crane Bag Book of
  Irish Studies* (see above).
Interview, in Monie Begley, *Rambles in Ireland*,
  Greenwich, Conn., 1977, pp. 159–79
Interviews, with Brian Donnelly and Edward Broadbridge,
  in Broadbridge (ed.), 1977 (see below)
'A Raindrop on a Thorn', with Robert Druce, *Dutch Quarterly
  Review*, vol. 9, 1978, pp. 24–37
John Haffenden, 'Meeting Seamus Heaney', *London
  Magazine*, June 1979, pp. 5–28. Reprinted in *Viewpoints:
  Poets in Conversation*, London, 1981, pp. 57–75
Denis O'Driscoll, 'In The Mid-Course of His Life', *Hibernia*,
  11 October 1979, p. 13
John Silverlight, 'Brooding Images', *Observer*, 11 November
  1979, p. 37
Interview, with James Randall, *Ploughshares*, 5:3, 1979,
  pp. 7–22
'Talk', with Seamus Deane, *New York Times Book Review*,
  2 December 1979, pp. 47–8
Interview, with Frank Kinahan, *Critical Inquiry*, 8:3, Spring
  1982, pp. 405–14

Fintan O'Toole, 'Heaney's Sweeney', *Irish Tribune*,
20 November 1983, p. 12
Fintan O'Toole, 'A Pilgrim's Progress', *Irish Tribune*,
30 September 1984, pp. 2, 6
Bel Mooney, 'Poet, pilgrim, fugitive . . .', *The Times*,
11 October 1984, p. 8

About Seamus Heaney

Books

Broadbridge, Edward (ed.), *Seamus Heaney*, Copenhagen,
1977
Buttel, Robert, *Seamus Heaney*, Lewisburg, Pa., 1975
Curtis, Tony (ed.), *The Art of Seamus Heaney*, Bridgend,
1982: revised, enlarged edition, 1985
Morrison, Blake, *Seamus Heaney*, London, 1982

Articles and reviews

Alvarez, A., 'A Fine Way With the Language' (on *Field
Work*), *New York Review of Books*, 6 March 1980,
pp. 16–17
Bloom, Harold, 'The voice of kinship' (on *Field Work*), *Times
Literary Supplement*, 8 February 1980, pp. 137–8
Carson, Ciaran, 'Escaped from the Massacre?' (on *North*),
The Honest Ulsterman, 50, Winter 1975, pp. 183–6
Deane, Seamus, 'Seamus Heaney: the Timorous and the
Bold', in *Celtic Revivals*, London, 1985, pp. 174–86
Dodsworth, Martin, 'Under duress' (on *North*), *Guardian*,
12 June 1975, p. 9
Foster, John Wilson, 'The Poetry of Seamus Heaney',
Critical Quarterly, 16:1, Spring 1974, pp. 35–48
Foster, John Wilson, 'Seamus Heaney's "A Lough Neagh
Sequence": Sources and Motifs', *Eire–Ireland*, 12:2,
Summer 1977, pp. 138–42
Longley, Edna, 'Fire and Air' (some remarks on *North*),
The Honest Ulsterman, 50, Winter 1975, pp. 54–8. See also
her essay on *North* in Curtis (ed.)

McGuinness, Arthur E., 'The Craft of Diction: Revision in Seamus Heaney's Poems', in Maurice Harmon (ed.), *Image and Illusion: Anglo-Irish Literature and Its Contexts*, Portmarnock, 1979, pp. 62–91

Miller, Karl, 'Opinion', the *Review*, 27–8, Autumn–Winter 1971–2, pp. 41–52

Morrison, Blake, 'Encounters with familiar ghosts' (on *Station Island*), *Times Literary Supplement*, 19 October 1984, pp. 1191–2

Murphy, Richard, 'Poetry and Terror' (on *North*), *New York Review of Books*, 30 September 1976, pp. 38–40

O'Brien, Conor Cruise, 'A slow north-east wind' (on *North*), *Listener*, 25 September 1975, pp. 404–5

Ricks, Christopher, 'The Mouth, the Meal and the Book' (on *Field Work*), *London Review of Books*, 8 November 1979, pp. 4–5

Schmidt, A. V. C., '"Darkness Echoing": Reflections on the Return of Mythopoeia in Some Recent Poems of Geoffrey Hill and Seamus Heaney', *Review of English Studies*, NS xxxvi, 142, 1985, pp. 199–225

Stallworthy, Jon, 'The Poet as Archaeologist: W. B. Yeats and Seamus Heaney', *Review of English Studies*, NS xxxiii, 130, 1982, pp. 158–74

Vendler, Helen, 'The Music of What Happens', *New Yorker*, 28 September 1981, pp. 146–57

Vendler, Helen, 'Echo Soundings, Searches, Probes' (on *Station Island*), *New Yorker*, 23 September 1985, pp. 108, 111–16

Books containing incidental material on Heaney

Bailey, Anthony, *Acts of Union: Reports on Ireland 1973–79*, London, 1980

Brown, Terence, *Northern Voices: Poets from Ulster*, Dublin, 1975

Devlin, Polly, *All Of Us There*, London, 1983

Dunn, Douglas (ed.), *Two Decades of Irish Writing*, Manchester, 1975

Ricks, Christopher, *The Force of Poetry*, Oxford, 1984

Trotter, David, *The Making of the Reader*, London, 1983

Index

Gabbey, Alan, 21
'Gifts of Rain', 84–5, 86, 89
'Girls Bathing, Galway 1965', 64
'Glanmore Sonnets', 90, 115, 142–9
Glob, P. V., 28, 60, 77, 78, 95, 99, 113, 114–15, 118
'The God in the Tree', 173
Goya, Francisco José de, 99, 108
'The Grauballe Man', 97, 99, 114–15
Graves, Robert, 47, 170–1
Gravities, 53
Grey, Lord, 100, 121
'The Group', 21–2

Haffenden, John, 100–1, 127, 180
Hailstones, 11
Hardy, Thomas, 139, 157
Harvard University, 37–8
'The Harvest Bow', 149–51
Hass, Robert, 38
Heaney, Agnes, 161
Heaney, Catherine Ann, 24
Heaney, Christopher, 12, 52
Heaney, Christopher, 24
Heaney, Margaret Kathleen, 11, 52
Heaney, Marie, 12–13, 24
Heaney, Mary, 12
Heaney, Michael, 24
Heaney, Patrick, 11–12, 52
Hedge School, 147
'Hercules and Antaeus', 100–1, 114
'The Hermit', 173
Hewitt, John, 19, 24
'High Summer', 139
Hill, Geoffrey, 30, 96
Hobsbaum, Philip, 21–2, 23, 25, 44
Holland, Mary, 22

'Holly', 175
'Homecomings', 141
The Honest Ulsterman, 21–2, 34
Hopkins, Gerard Manley, 18, 44, 100, 107
Horace, 100
Hughes, Francis, 162
Hughes, Olwyn, 33
Hughes, Ted, 19, 21, 33, 39, 44, 45–6, 47, 49, 59, 61, 67, 148
Hume, John, 17

Imprint (radio programme), 35, 36
'In the Beech', 175, 176
'In Gallarus Oratory', 60, 64
'In Illo Tempore', 175, 178
'Intimidation', 28, 29
IRA, 26, 29, 116, 137, 162
'Iron Spike', 157

Jarrell, Randall, 57
John of the Cross, St, 163, 165
Jones, David, 96, 112, 133
Joyce, James, 18, 74, 82, 83, 99, 111, 145, 148, 156, 163, 166, 167–8, 169, 173, 177
Jung, C. G., 62

Kavanagh, Patrick, 20, 47, 49, 53, 98, 100, 143, 159, 161, 167
Keats, John, 18, 150
Keenan, Terry, 161
Kelly, Luke, 27
Kinahan, Frank, 11, 107, 127, 128
King, Henry, 139
'The King of the Ditchbacks', 153–4, 172
Kinsella, Thomas, 19
'Kinship', 97, 100, 103–4, 106, 118–20